Revised and Ev
Allen & Mike's
TELEMARK TIPS

123 amazing tips to improve your tele-skiing

It's cosmic!

Allen O'Bannon
&
Mike Clelland!

FALCONGUIDES ®

GUILFORD, CONNECTICUT
HELENA, MONTANA

AN IMPRINT OF THE GLOBE PEQUOT PRESS

FALCONGUIDES®

Illustrations by Mike Clelland!

Library of Congress Cataloging-in-Publication Data
O'Bannon, Allen.
   Allen & Mike's really cool telemark tips / Allen O'Bannon, Mike Clelland. – 2nd ed.
      p. cm. – (A Falcon guide)
   ISBN-13: 978-0-7627-4586-9
   1. Telemark (Skiing) I. Clelland, Mike. II. Clelland, Mike. III. Title.
   GV854.9.T44O33 2008
   796.93–dc22

                                        2008011144

Printed in the United States of America
10 9 8 7 6 5 4 3 2 1

Contents

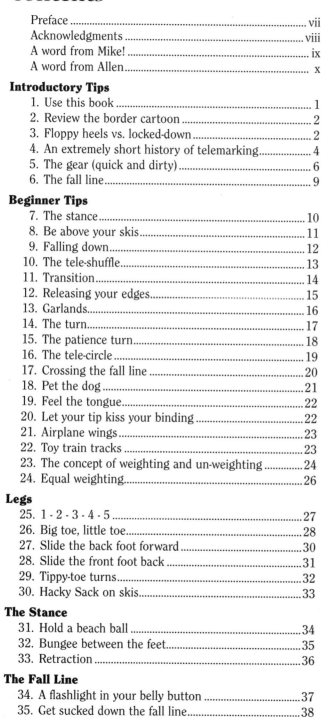

Preface

When I talk to people who own the original tele-tips book, I am always amazed at how many tell me it was how they learned to telemark or how much it helped their skiing. Heck, I guess we accomplished what we set out to do, and I just wanted to thank all those who have shared their passion for skiing (and our book) with us. I also want to thank Mike for the inspiration behind the book. Like a preacher, he truly wants to spread the word.

Things have changed a lot since we wrote the first version of this book, and it's far past the time for an update. We have tried our best to present the latest techniques while preserving the tips that are still relevant. Mike has taken a bigger lead in writing tips as well as illustrating, and I have stayed away from drawing entirely to keep the book fun and interesting. We hope you find it as enjoyable and helpful as the first one—we certainly enjoyed researching it. Remember to get away from the lifts from time to time to enjoy the freedom and beauty of free-heeling it in the backcountry. Thanks.

Tele on!

Allen O'Bannon

Acknowledgments

These are the floppy-heeled pals who contributed to this book:

Rich "Agro-C" Rinaldi, Clair "Sneaky" Yost, Don "The Steeps" Sharaf, Chris "Riding Porpoises" Lander, K. K. "Toy Train" Cool Day, Erika "Punch Downhill" Eschholz, Jim Ferguson, Margaret "Ski the Trees" Thompson, Mitch "I'd rather be climbing" Ross, Angela "Knees Together" Patnode, Bill "Equal Weight" Mohrwinkel, Tracy Jane "The Right Equipment" Young, Mark Johnson, Tony Jewell, Deb Payne, Tori Hederman, Brad Sawtell, Molly "Tray" Absolon, Kristin "Unweight" McInaney, Christian Beckwith, Mark Bergstrom, Nina Cook, Greg Collins, Willy "Turn Faster" Peebottle, Marc Kessler, Sarah Levesen, Bill "Butt Cheeks" Zell, Matt Mitchel, Mindy Breen, Jeff Newsome, Lynn "Bounce" Morrison, Andy "Bouncy Bouncy" Wallbert, Naheed "Ski with her if you can" Hendersen, Scott McGee, some lady from New Hampshire, Connely "3rd Dimension" Brown, Cotton T-shirt Ned, Brien "How to Fall" Sheedy, everybody at the NOLS Idaho winter base, and all the other powder hounds that drop the knee and not the bomb.

Lastly, a big huge thanks to Erica Linnel, who let us tag around with her on the ski slopes, answered our questions, and generally added to our store of knowledge. It's not every day you find someone willing to share all they know with you.

A word from Mike!

There are millions of free-heel athletes out there who are oodles better at the telemark turn than I'll ever be. The fact is, I ain't that great of a tele-skier. It's only through lots of years of hard work that I've gotten to the point I'm at today. I'm not really a ski instructor either. I do work for an outdoor school a few weeks each winter, but mostly we teach winter camping, not telemarking.

What I am is a cartoonist and ski bum. My formative years were spent reading *MAD* magazine, and now that's how I'm forever doomed to draw. My illustration style looks goofy, and the goofier the better! In this book I've worked hard to transpose the very subtle mechanics of telemark skiing into an overtly visual and berserk cartoon-a-rama. My goal was to give you something concrete to latch onto in the midst of all these sometimes esoteric skiing skills.

You'll probably notice my editorializing in these pages. I like to get low in my turn, I prefer the backcountry to chairlifts, and I love skiing powder. And I still love my old leather boots, plus they're fun to draw. There is an inherent beauty in those smelly old leathers that just can't be matched by my new plastic monstrosities. A majority of the cartoons in this book reflect this truism.

I started tele-skiing in 1987, and I still draw these cartoons to match that era of wool pants and gaiters. That said, no illustration is complete without some drips of sweat and "Boing!" marks. I hope these drawings make it clear that I love to ski!

Please don't get all high-and-mighty and serious about this book. These cartoons are meant to convey some helpful hints in an extremely caricatured way, which means that there is nothing subtle here! Don't think you're some kind of smarty-pants just because you spot some little flaw in the technique of these cartoon skiers. I hope these drawings provide an easy-to-remember visual hook that'll help you put these tips to use. I encourage you to enjoy this book, and hopefully it'll improve your tele-skiing too!

Enough said,

Mike!

A word from Allen

This book is our attempt to help you improve your skiing. I must admit that originally I was skeptical about the idea of writing a ski tips book–not because I didn't think it would be fun or useful (or because I didn't think we would achieve fame and fortune), but rather because skiing is such a hard thing to teach. One person's key to success doesn't work for someone else–often because that someone else is too busy struggling with some uncooperative part of their anatomy to comprehend the valuable advice just given them. It's all they can do to respond "uh-huh."

The key to learning a dynamic sport like skiing is to spend a lot of time on skis. As instructors, we try to give folks tips on what they should do next, based on where they're at in their skill development. But let's face it: If you're not ready for a particular tip, then all you really want to do is spend time on your skis and keep your butt off the snow. Once in a while, though, we manage to give someone the right tip at just the right time, and off they go—totally satisfied and shredding at a new level. And that's what teaching is all about.

So I figured if we just filled this book with a variety of tips that worked for a variety of people, we might come up with something useful—not just for beginning and intermediate skiers, but also for some of those burnt-out instructors who are in need of some fresh air. And aside from all that, I knew that with Mike's illustrations, the book would at the very least be entertaining.

I learned to telemark at the advanced age of twenty-three and taught telemarking for many years. Through this experience I have come to realize that there are two basic fundamentals hopeful free-heelers must master. The first is maintaining balance while moving. Anyone can stand still on one leg, but to do it while moving is a different story, and mastering this skill takes some of us longer than others. The best way to get the dynamic balance required is to simply spend time on skis gliding about. You don't necessarily need to be doing turns downhill—just kicking and gliding along in the flats will help. Indeed, I try to convince my students to spend as much time as possible on their skis because the more comfortable you are with those long pointy things on your feet, the better you will be at controlling them.

The second fundamental is maintaining the correct body position. It is virtually impossible to telemark if all your body can do is stand up straight. You need to be able to bend those knees and drop into those turns! Practice holding this position while doing straight runs on mellow terrain, and eventually some muscle memory will kick in. You can spice up this routine by switching lead skis as you are moving, and by bending even further at the knees to see how low you can go.

If you are new to skiing, you may want to start out on the packed slopes of a ski area rather than in the backcountry. The packed snow will make it easier to concentrate on the basics, and the lift service will allow you much more time to work on your downhill technique.

A.O.

1 Use this book

This book isn't designed to languish on your coffee table, it's meant to be used! Put it in your pack and bring it along when you're skiing. This book is nothing more than a bunch of little tips meant to help you improve your telemark skiing, so don't expect it to give you a methodical step-by-step progression into the tele-turn. We'll leave that to Paul Parker's excellent book, *Free Heel Skiing*. Rather, just flip through this book and find those tips most relevant to you. Study the ones that you like and then practice, practice, practice! There's a chapter at the end of the book that points out some common mistakes; it will guide you to the numbered tips that can help you fix these errors in technique. So if any of these problems seem painfully familiar, simply turn to the appropriate tip for help. And, most importantly, don't forget to have fun!

② Review the border cartoon

The little flip-art cartoon along the book's border shows a pretty darned accurate tele-skier rippin' it up. Use this as a learning tool. As you improve, all you need to do is flip the pages faster to quicken up the rhythm, just like real life.

③ Floppy heels vs. locked-down

Do you want to learn the telemark turn? Are you coming from a background of alpine skiing? If so, right on! But get ready to be a beginner all over again—don't worry, being a greenhorn is good for the soul.

This isn't a rule, but the lifelong alpine skier trying to telemark for the first time might get a tad frustrated. These folks are locked into a specific muscle memory that can be dreadful when applied to tele-gear. Alpine skis are equipped with power steering, but tele-gear requires an extra degree of elegance and grace. There are some fundamental differences between the alpine and telemark turn, and there are pros and cons to each. If you feel that alpine skiing is getting a little stale and you're ready to evolve, free-heel gear may be just the challenge you're looking for. Plus, there is a wonderful freedom that comes with a floppy heel. The main advantage is that you can travel beyond the limitations of the lift-served resorts. Free your heel, and your soul will follow.

Some tele-facts:

- You might fall more often.
- You might never go as fast as your alpine friends.
- You use a few different muscles in your legs.
- Tele-skiing offers new and fun challenges.
- Tele-skiers are always being maligned. (Bring it on!)
- When you rip a better line than your alpine friends, you know who gets the respect.
- Telemark skiing is amazingly beautiful!

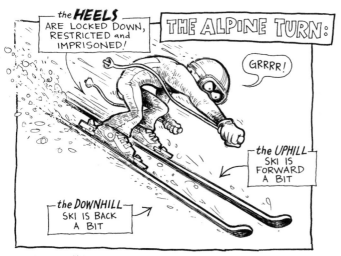

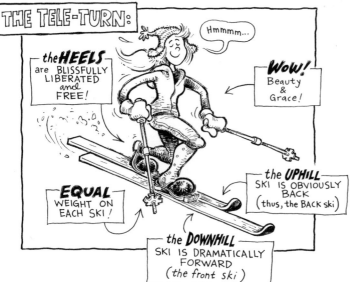

ancient
NORWAY

4 An extremely short history of telemarking

In the old days, skiing was more utilitarian in nature than sport. People skied with one pole (known as a *lurk*) in order to have one arm free for carrying groceries or, when necessary, rescuing babies. Skis made of solid wood were long, skinny, and straight. Boots were normally attached to the ski by only the toe. In the mid-1800s, a fellow by the name of Sondre Norheim from the District of Telemark in Norway helped to popularize skiing and the telemark turn. He also introduced shorter skis that not only had side cut, but also were mounted with a type of cable binding made of twisted willow roots.

In the 1970s, telemarking began to catch on in the United States. The skis were skinny, the poles were tall, and the boots were low-cut and made of leather. Telemarking was a fringy alternative to downhill resort skiing. The lightweight gear and free heel allowed people to go beyond the lift lines and into the backcountry to ski the fluffy stuff. With time, skis began to get wider and the original floppy boots got taller and stiffer. The three pin bindings that had been de rigueur were phased out in favor of cable bindings once again. Free-heelers were often referred to as pin-heads, pinners, or maggots. The unenlightened would even attempt to impose their power-steering dogma with verbiage like "Half a binding, half a brain" and "Free the heel, plant the face." However, we tele-skiers persevered.

Telemarking
comes to America
(70's & 80's)

The '90s brought
plastic boots, and they completely revolutionized
telemark skiing. Not only did these big boots provide more
control, but they also made it a whole lot easier to learn the
tele-turn. As the sport became increasingly mainstream, more
and more gear companies got into the act. Bigger boots meant
bigger skis, and these required extra-beefy bindings just to
hold all the massive stuff together. The revolution continued
with skis: They kept getting fatter, and by the new millennium
they were so fat that they are now referred to as low fat, mid
fat, fat, and super fat. Add some dramatic side cut to the actual
shape of the skis, and it gets easier to learn and even quicker
to excel. It's hard to comprehend how revolutionary a single
decade can be for a sport that was once the domain of a few
fringe pin-heads.

Combine all these powerhouse advancements
in gear together, and it has become dramatically easier for the beginning tele-skier to
catapult from gumby to expert. There is a
new breed of tele-skier out there who has
never suffered the long learning curve
mandated by the leather boots and
skinny skis. It's these folks who are
changing the sport in spectacular
ways. We (Allen & Mike!) aren't in
our twenties anymore, or our thirties
either, and it's hard to keep up with
these new powerhouse tele-gods—now
they are teaching us!

after the
revolution

5 The gear (quick and dirty)

A friend showed up at my door the other day all excited about the great deal he just got on a pair of skis. However, when he showed me what he'd bought, all I could do was shake my head in sadness—too skinny, too long, and too stiff. While these skis might have been used for telemarking back in the days of the dinosaurs, they would only prolong his misery when he was learning to turn. Skis like that would be fine for touring across golf courses in Minnesota, but if you want to turn, then get skis that turn. Stay away from cross-country skis and gear that "does it all." If making telemark turns is a new challenge for you, start off with the right type of equipment.

Skis: The market is awash in awesome tele-skis. Getting brand-new high-performance skis is easy as long as you haven't maxed out your credit card. If, on the other hand, your pocketbook dictates you shop at the thrift store, look for boards that are

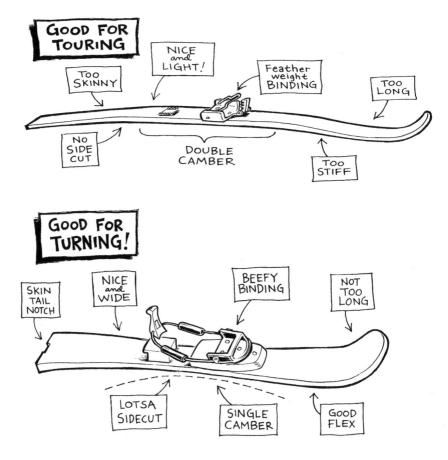

wide. An old pair of tele-skis, or even alpine boards mounted with free-heel bindings, is a great (and cheap) way to start out in the sport. Don't worry about high-performance skis; these can wait until you're ready for high-performance turns. For now, any wide and easy-flexing skis will turn just fine.

Skis that are skinny and stiff and have a groove down the middle are made for touring, not downhill performance. In fact, these skis are almost impossible to turn. Touring skis are double-cambered and have a wax pocket. When squeezed together in the middle, a gap will exist between the bases under the foot. Tele-skis are single camber and are easy to squeeze together.

Side cut: All modern telemark skis are equipped with some degree of side cut, which means they're wider at the tip and tail and thinner at the waist. Some skis have minimal side cut, while others, such as the modern *shaped* skis (parabolic or hourglass), have a really dramatic side cut. This curvy shape really gets those skis to turn, and they are amazingly responsive and fun! The parabolic side cut can make for some mind-bogglingly quick turns with relatively little effort. A curved ski likes to make a curved line in the snow. Shaped skis need less weighting and un-weighting to get them to perform, and this is something new compared to the long straight skis of a previous era. Shaped skis like to be weighted all the time, and this requires consistent pressure from the driver.

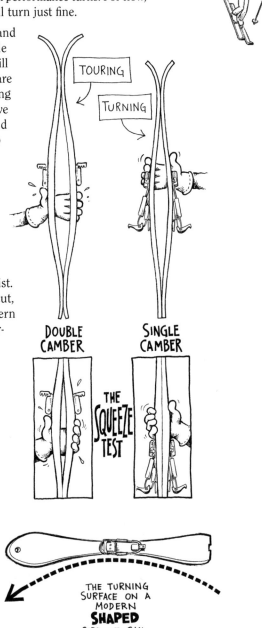

A noteworthy benefit of curvy skis is that beginners can hop on a pair of them and vault up the ladder toward expert in a way that would have once-upon-a-time been impossible.

Boots: Plastic boots are the gold standard in tele-skiing. The bigger and heavier the boot, the more performance and *oomph* they deliver. Monstrous boots are powerful tools for aggressive skiing in-bounds with the help of a chairlift. But, unless you have legs of steel, these same boots can exhaust you on a long day in the backcountry. Still, plenty of tele-skiers schlep their hulking boots up long skin tracks, and if they've got the big guns to do it, then more power to 'em.

BIG BOOT
(in-bounds & power)

BACKCOUNTRY
(lighter for touring)

LEATHER
(quaint & comfy)

Backcountry boots are smaller, lighter, and more flexible. They are more nimble for a long tour into the mountains to find that perfect powder bowl. These boots can feel like they limit your performance, but with a little extra skill refinement from the driver, they work great. Watch out for little boots that are designed more for touring than turning. It's tricky in this age of specialization to find one piece of gear that does it all.

If you want to get back to the roots of tele-skiing, try skiing an old pair of leather boots—they are easy to find at any garage sale in a ski town. It's a fun challenge, and it'll really make you appreciate those tele-skiers of years past. These boots require an extra level of proficiency and finesse. If you spend even a little time in a pair of flimsy leathers, you'll be required to find a delicate balance point, and you'll truly benefit when you switch back to your big plastics.

6 The fall line

If you rolled a beach ball down a ski slope, the line it would take as it travels is called the *fall line*. The ball only wants to go one way: It wants to follow the path of least resistance and surrender to the pull of gravity. This is what skiing is all about—embracing gravity. This term gets used a lot in these pages, and it's crucial to be able to visualize this invisible line in the snow. The essence of the ski experience is to gracefully move down the fall line.

Turns are used to check your speed and provide you with a sense of control. It's essential to always have your upper body facing down the fall line. This makes for quicker turns because you only have to maneuver half your body (the lower half) across and through the fall line.

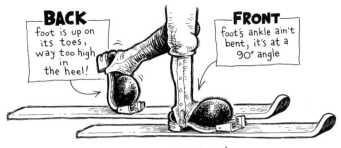

BACK
foot is up on its toes, way too high in the heel!

FRONT
foot's ankle ain't bent, it's at a 90° angle

LOUSY STANCE!

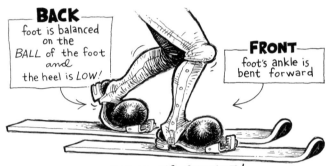

BACK
foot is balanced on the BALL of the foot *and* the heel is LOW!

FRONT
foot's ankle is bent forward

FABULOUS STANCE!

7 The stance

The entirety of telemark skiing is utterly dependent on this beautiful *stance*. Where your feet are and how you stand on 'em is the heart and soul of the telemark position. It's all based on an athletic stance—a nice, stable body position with your feet apart, knees bent, shoulders low, and your hands out in front of your body. Think of a soccer goalie getting ready to block a penalty kick; it's this stable pose you want to aim for. You want to be both loose and ready to spring into action. This secure position defines the tele-stance.

Let's start with the *downhill* foot, also known as the *outside, lead,* or *front* foot. Your knee should be directly above the toes of your front foot. Both the ankle and knee should be bent, giving you a nice forward cant. Your front boot will be hidden from view by your knee when you are in a good tele-position.

Now for the *uphill* foot, also known as the *inside, trailing,* or *back* foot. This foot is bent at the baffle of the boot with the heel lifted slightly off the back ski. You support half your weight on this foot, so stand firmly on the ball of the foot, not on your tippy-toes. Don't let the knees get too spread out. You should feel nimble, loose, and ready to go in this customized athletic stance.

Speech bubbles in image 2:

BACK — heel should be directly below your bung-hole...

FRONT — knee should be directly over your front toes!

These rules still apply in a **LOW** BODY POSITION!

8 Be above your skis

The position of your upper body is essential for a true telemark stance. You *always* want to be directly above your skis, because it's your body weight that controls them. If they get out from under you, there's no way to weight 'em. It's common for beginners to depend too much on the front foot, steering the ski with a straight leg. The front foot requires a nice bend in the ankle, enough that it creates firm pressure in the shin of the boot.

Alas, it's that pesky back foot that seems to demand the most attention. Ignore it, and it'll just trail along behind you like the neighbor's dog. The telemark experience requires keeping the back foot directly under you so your weight can transfer to the ski. This, more than anything else, is the bane of the strong alpine skier new to the telemark turn. The heel (or the Achilles, to be more exact) of your back foot needs to be targeted under your butt. If instead your calf muscle is positioned below your butt, your back foot is too far back. Whether your stance is nice and tall or scrunched low, these rules don't change. If you get low, stay compact so the weight stays above your skis. If you make the mistake of getting too spread out, you lose the power of your body weight transferring to the ski's surface.

SHORT FALL

OY!

UPHILL FALL

well padded area

9 Falling down

It goes without saying that a basic goal in skiing is to avoid falling down. However, the reality is that it's inevitable. Besides, there are advantages to falling down—for one thing, it's a surefire way to stop—so it's worth knowing how to do it right. You want to avoid going plop in a way that could blow out a knee or smash your head. Being able to stop instantly is very important when you find yourself out of control or when a tree jumps out of nowhere into your path. Another good thing about falling down is that it doesn't take a lot of practice, so you can feel successful right away.

The best way to fall down is to fall off to one side (usually uphill) and land on your butt, since that's where most of the padding is. To get up again, position your skis downhill and across the fall line, then push your weight up over the top of them. In deep powder it helps to lay your poles on the snow and push off of them.

EXTRA LONG FALLING DISTANCE!

floppy heels!

Poorly padded area

DOWNHILL FALL

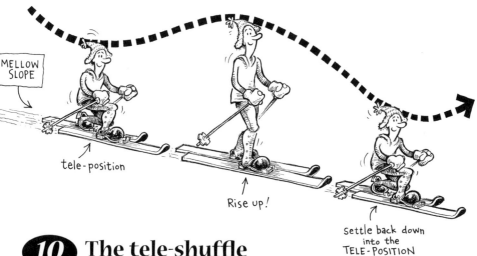

MELLOW
SLOPE

tele-position

Rise up!

settle back down
into the
TELE-POSITION

(10) **The tele-shuffle**

    Here's the most fundamental tip in the book. This simple exercise reinforces the dependability of the telemark stance, and it should be practiced until you have it ingrained in your memory. Find a mellow slope (no need to bring fear into the equation) and ski slowly across it. As you ski across, gently drop into the tele-position. Think about smoothly sinking down from a nice athletic stance into your tele-position, *downhill* foot *forward*. Next, gently rise back up to an athletic stance, then sink back down into that same tele-position. Embrace the stability and beauty of the telemark pose, and allow yourself to feel comfortable and steady as you glide across the snow. Focus on a constant fluid motion, rising up and settling back down. Practice in both directions across the slope.

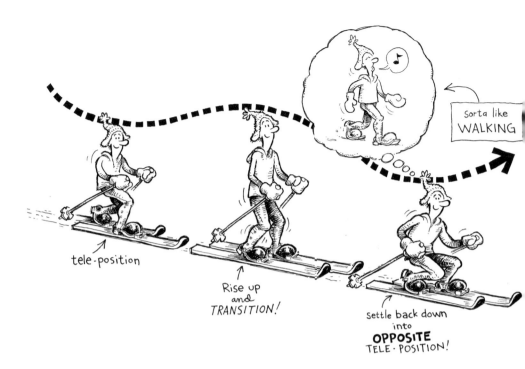

tele-position

Rise up
and
TRANSITION!

Settle back down
into
OPPOSITE
TELE·POSITION!

Sorta like
WALKING

⑪ Transition

Once you master the tele-shuffle, you're ready for the transition. Cross the same slope you were on before, but now *switch the lead foot* each time you drop back down into the tele-position. Think *extension* as you rise up and *compression* as you sink down. It's during the transition that your body will be tallest, the *up* part of the subtle up and down. This is called the *straight-run* telemark, and it's similar to walking, as you put one foot in front of the other. But unlike walking, there's an equal *push and pull* in the movement of the two skis, making the skis *smear* past each other with identical pressure. Find a nice smooth rhythm, and don't pause in between steps—each step should smoothly flow from the one before. Most importantly, focus on the equal and consistent weighting of each ski. This equal weighting is the heart and soul of the majority of the tips in this book, so embrace this good habit early. Again, practice in both directions across the slope.

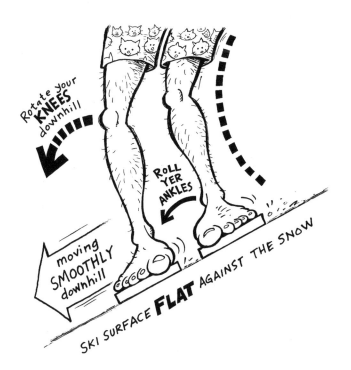

⑫ Releasing your edges

Standing on skis on a slope requires that you know this one essential trick: positioning your skis perpendicular to the fall line. To do this, you'll need to stand with the uphill edges of your skis dug into the slope so they grab the snow. Easy enough, right?

Now, from this stable standing position, roll your knees downhill, and let those edges lose their bite. As your skis flatten against the snow, you'll start sliding downhill. You have just learned how to *release your edges* and slip down the slope– congratulations! This is called *side-slipping,* and it can be done in either a parallel or tele-stance. Play with this as you slide downhill, and you'll quickly realize you can perform this trick smoothly and with control. You can go slow or fast just by the position of your edges against the snow. This basic technique will come into play as you perfect your skills.

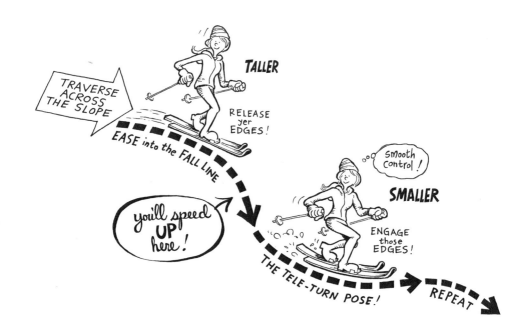

13 Garlands

Making the transition from one turn to another requires you to release the edges of your skis and let them come into the fall line. You then gradually pressure them (and engage the edges) to create the next turn. But, if you can't release the edges smoothly, you wind up with a herky-jerky transition. Practice doing a traverse across a gentle slope and dropping into the tele-stance, then *edge* and *pressure* those skis into the slope just enough to really feel the power of the stance. Before you come to a stop, gently rise up and let your skis seek the fall line again. Keep repeating this as you traverse across the slope—engage your edges, slow down and turn across the fall line, then release, start to come back into the fall line, and engage the edges again. This is called a *garland,* and the track you leave in the snow will be a gentle series of arc-shaped curves. Practice traversing both ways across the slope, and think about how smooth you can make it all feel.

An important part of this tip is to make sure your upper body is facing downhill the whole time. This simple act will be hugely beneficial in the long run because it develops strong body position.

The INITIATION

Rise up

Release my edges

The TRANSITION →
(the skis pass each other)

New lead ski

Settle a little lower

The FINISH

14 The turn

The telemark turn has three distinct parts: the *initiation*, the *transition*, and the *finish*.

Once again, let's start by crossing that same mellow slope, traversing in a tele-position with your downhill leg in front. Point your upper body downhill, gently rise up, and rotate your knees in the direction you want to turn; this will release your edges and your skis will seek the fall line. This is the *initiation* phase.

Your skis will begin to point downhill, and it's in this magic moment that you *switch the lead ski* by sliding the back ski forward. Make the skis *smear* past each other with identical pressure. This is the *transition* phase, and in the beginning it might happen quickly. It's during the transition that your body will be tallest, the *up* part of the subtle up and down.

Finally, that back ski will push ahead into its new position out front. Think about pressuring both skis into the turn and feel them arc around. This phase is the *finish,* and you should let yourself settle into this lowest part of the turn. Everything concludes with your skis edging across the fall line. This part of the turning action lets you dump some speed as well, so if you're going too fast and it gets scary, just allow yourself to feel how the finish can slow you down.

Now all you have to do is gently rise up, release your edges, and start over again.

yawn...

RISE UP

Simply allow the skis to seek the FALL LINE

SINK DOWN

15 The patience turn

If you are having trouble releasing your edges and getting the feel for the transition, or if you just can't get into the fall line, this exercise will help. It's also an easy way to begin linking turns together. Do this drill on a mellow slope, and let the fall line do the work.

Start with a gentle traverse, simply allowing the skis to seek the fall line. *Do nothing*—just relax and stand there, and let those skis naturally make a gentle turn in the direction of gravity. Gently *release your edges* by simply allowing both skis to ride flat on the snow so the edges aren't grabbing. Wait until your skis are pointing straight downhill and into the fall line; you'll feel yourself speed up a little. Now, settle down into the tele-turn position, *engage your edges,* and steer those skis in the same gentle arc. You complete the turn by coming across the fall line and slowing down.

Next, do it again in the other direction. As you get more comfortable, you can let it all flow together a little faster. Instead of just letting gravity start the turn, you can initiate it by steering yourself toward the fall line.

16 The tele-circle

Here's another good practice drill. Find a nice mellow slope with an open and consistent bit of steepness. Set yourself up in the tele-stance with your downhill leg forward and uphill leg back, just like the tele-traverse. Start at the top of a great big circle, right at 12 o'clock. The idea here is to scribe part of the circle with your skis. As you start down, gently *initiate* the turn by pointing your knees and skis in the direction of the circle. Keep your upper body facing down the fall line. You should ride smoothly through the fall line and *transition* at 9 o'clock, then *finish* the turn at 6 o'clock. You'll ease to a stop at around 4 o'clock. Complete the circle by herring-boning back up the slope to 12 o'clock, and start all over again. Do this multiple times, smoothing it all out so each circle flows into the next one. You should end up with a nice rounded groove in the snow; use this as a track for each consecutive turn.

If this feels like it's too much, just go for an easy start. Enter the circle at around 8 o'clock from the outside, and concentrate on making your motions nice and smooth. Repeat this until you feel like you can comfortably get up to the 12 o'clock starting position.

Switch directions and work on the same stuff going the other way around the clock. Have someone stand at the bottom of the circle and review your technique. Remember to keep your body facing downhill throughout the entirety of the turn.

THE
FALL
LINE

17   Crossing the fall line

If you actually pointed your skis straight down the fall line and let gravity take over, you could easily reach Mach speeds, even on the bunny slope. You might find the excess velocity a bit intimidating. Fortunately, we can control our speed. Turns provide us speed control and maneuverability as we traverse back and forth *across the fall line*.

It's in the deepest point of each tele-turn that our skis will actually be crossing the fall line. As your skis and feet swing around in the curving shape of each turn, your upper body should stay in the fall line, and your eyes should be directed straight down this imaginary line. This upper-body position helps maximize what we can do with our skis.

18 Pet the dog

This simple drill works great to get your body facing downhill. Sink into your tele-stance and pet a nice big Labrador trotting along on your downhill side. Pet him (or her) with your uphill hand. This forces you to rotate those shoulders and hips down the hill. Here's a good warm-up for this tip: Just pet your own knee instead of the invisible dog. Reach your *uphill hand* around, and pat your *downhill knee* in the low point of each tele-turn.

UPHILL HAND

19 Feel the tongue

To get your front foot in the correct tele-position, you'll want to feel some pressure on the front of your shin against the tongue of your boot. If you are *not* feeling the

FEEL IT!

PRESSURE
against
TONGUE!

tongue, then you either need to buckle your boots or bend your ankles. It's this flexing at the ankles that gets you into the front of your boot—it gets you bending at the knees without sitting back over the tails of the skis. If you taped a quarter on the inside of each tongue, at the end of the day, George Washington would be imprinted on your shins.

You definitely don't want to feel the opposite sensation, pressure on the back of your calf. This means your front leg is too straight. The only way to feel the pressure from your tongue is to bend forward at the ankle.

20 Let your tip kiss your binding

If you just can't get your first true tele-turn, you might need to try something overly exaggerated. This tip could help. When you're working on getting that feel for the tele-position, think

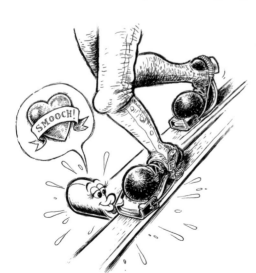

SMOOCH!

of letting your ski tip "kiss" the binding of the other ski at the low point (compression) of each turn. While this position is going to be too spread out compared to the stance of an advanced skier, it's a nice visual way for you to work on the basic position because you can just look down and see it. After you master this overly excessive pose, make sure to *un-learn* it by standing up a little taller and cinching those feet in a little tighter. The boot-to-binding kiss was the way some old-timers learned with low leather boots back in the '80s.

21 Airplane wings

This is a great mental and visual exercise that helps beginners smooth out the herky-jerky motions of the upper body. Imagine yourself with airplane wings carefully balanced on your shoulders. Ski without poles, and put your arms straight out and pretend you're an airplane. The key to a safe flight is to keep your aircraft pointed down the hill. Your legs will be doing all the work, so try to keep your upper body quiet and smooth. The airplane should move gracefully down the slope.

22 Toy train tracks

Do you freeze between turns, holding your compressed telemark position for a long traverse before you get the gumption to extend and turn again? If so, the solution is easy. Imagine you are riding on a toy train track. The track is made up of straight sections and curved sections. The novice skier will hold a long traverse on the straight tracks before committing to the next turn. The advanced skier, however, uses *only the curves,* simply rising and sinking into each turn as if the straight track simply didn't exist—each turn flows directly from the one before it. If you get frozen into position, all you need to do is remove the straight track and only ski the curves.

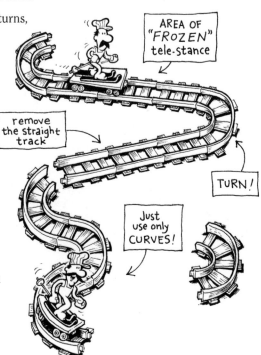

AREA OF "FROZEN" tele-stance

remove the straight track

TURN!

Just use only CURVES!

Scale sez: **150** lbs

Scale sez: **300** Lbs!

Scale sez: **0** Lbs.

(WEIGHTING) (UN-WEIGHTING)

23 The concept of weighting and unweighting

Skiing should be dynamic, with some beautiful motions beyond just the magical glide of your skis. Our little skier is shown here on a bathroom scale, weighing in at a fit 150 pounds. As long as he is standing still, the scale doesn't change.

Now suppose we glued that scale to his feet and got him bouncing on a trampoline. At his lowest point (compression) the scale reads 300 pounds, or double his static weight. That weighting creates some powerful energy in the trampoline, or in your skis. In the next instant he is shot up (extension), and at the highest point in his ride, he is un-weighting—the scale registers zero. So in a blink of an eye our skier goes from doubling his weight to zero gravity. This is a fundamental of skiing, even though this explanation is a bit exaggerated. Let's see what happens when we put those scales on our skis.

First, let's define camber. Set your skis flat on the ground and look at them. They should touch the floor at the tip and tail and rise up to a high point somewhere under the binding. This is known as *camber*. Now push down in the middle until they are perfectly flat on the floor, and then let go. What did they do? They snapped back up. We use this rebounding energy to help us turn.

When you come into a turn, if you sink down and aggressively *weight* your skis (compression), the camber gets pushed out, and this reversed shape creates a turning surface. Standing up again (extension) *un-weights* the skis and you achieve an instant of zero gravity; use that moment of upward trajectory to transition. Then as you weight the skis again, you force them into the next turn. This really comes into play in the steeps and in the bumps, in powder and in gloppy snow.

EACH
Scale sez:
0 lbs.

the Transition
(UN-WEIGHTING)
Extension

the TURN !
(WEIGHTING)
Compression

Scales say
150 EACH!
for a total of:
300 lbs.

24 Equal weighting

Look at our perfect tele-skier as he gently rides 'em: The bathroom scales for his front and back feet each read exactly 75 pounds. Each foot is balancing precisely half his body weight. This skill of equal weighting will do more to make you a perfect tele-skier than any other tip in this book.

Now look at our lame skier: He's only weighting his front ski while completely ignoring his back ski. He's setting himself up for disaster. On a hard-packed surface (like a ski area or back-country corn snow), he might manage to cheat like this and get down a slope, albeit wobbly. But this creates a problem: If you don't get enough weight on the back ski, it assumes you don't care and it'll go wherever it wants. This lack of control makes the back ski squirrelly. You may not know it, but a friend skiing behind you will be able to watch the un-weighted ski wobble and chatter.

PERFECT!

Scales say: **75** lbs. **EACH!**

As you do a turn, keep your up-hill boot under you, and push it through the turn. The problem won't get solved until you dramatically shift your weight to that back ski. This is a common mistake, and fortunately, this book has a bunch of specific tips calculated to help.

You might deceive yourself on a groomer thinking you've mastered the tele-turn, but you'll get spanked on a powder day. In the deep stuff, that un-weighted back ski is a source of frustration—and planted heads. The tip of the back ski will dive down in the soft snow, and the momentum of everything else will throw you forward, face first into the snow. For the deep stuff, it's incredibly important to have your weight evenly distributed over both skis so you can *float* on a single platform.

LAME...

FRONT Scale Sez: **149** lbs.

BACK Scale sez: **1** lb.

PARALLEL (Ewww!) **1.**

Just barely **2.**

A NICE STABLE TELE-POZE! *OH YEAH!* **3.**

slightly Too Wide **4.**

YIKES! gettin' SPREAD OUT! **5.**

25 1 - 2 - 3 - 4 - 5

The telemark foot position can be quantified with a simple number system. Check out the series: Number 1 is the parallel stance, and that's not a telemark position at all. Number 5 actually is a telemark position, but it's way too spread out to use your boots effectively. Right in the middle is number 3, the beautiful and stable position we dearly love, not too spread out, with palpable pressure in the tongue of the front boot and the back foot right under you so it can get actively weighted. Be aware that occasionally even the most skilled tele-skier will drift into the number 4 position, and that's okay. Just try to achieve that perfect number 3 pose with some consistency.

Have a trusted pal ski alongside you for a run. He or she can watch your turns and shout out the number you are doing. Alas, if "SIX!" is shouted, you've got some dreadful behavior to correct.

THREE!

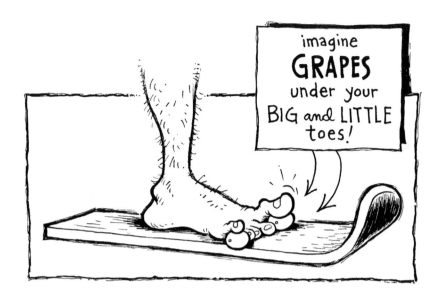

26 Big toe, little toe

      This is a surefire way to focus on your edging. Pretend you have grapes positioned under your big and little toes. When you are doing a turn, you want to squash the grape under your big toe with your downhill foot. With your uphill foot, you squash the grape under your little toe. Be aggressive with this

grape-flattening pressure because it's this action, from your toe to your ski, that makes those edges bite into the snow.

If you need to shift more weight to your back ski, direct your energy to the grape under the little toe of your back foot. Be forceful, and think about powering that edge hard into the snow. Celebrate your success with a glass of wine squeezed from your socks.

BIG TOE, LITTLE TOE transfers directly to the uphill EDGES!

27 Slide the back foot forward

The transition of the tele-turn should be a magical motion with equal energy transferred to each ski as they slide. But, sometimes we need a mental gimmick to help perfect our technique. This tip and the next are ways to focus on your transition.

As you end one turn, slide that rear foot forward into the next. Think about putting pressure on it as you move it forward. This will help you initiate the turn and set you up for a nice smooth transition. The tele-turn is a series of beautiful flowing motions, and your focus should be on moving forward. This is a nice, positive mental image for the beginner to focus on while on gentle terrain. For a smoother transition, think *back foot slides forward.*

28 Slide the front foot back

Now let's contradict the previous tip, since there are times when you want to flip the preceding mindset around. When skiing the steeps or a bump run, you want to snap through each transition really quickly. The front ski needs to slide quickly backward to its stable position under you. In reality, you should be pushing and pulling equally on each ski in the transition. It's the focus of your mental energy that changes. For a faster transition, think *front foot slides backward*.

KEEP them HEELS UP!

29 Tippy-toe turns

Try doing a nice long traverse on a gentle slope with *both heels* up off the skis. You'll immediately appreciate the advantage of being on the balls of the feet versus up on your tippy-toes. This tip helps you really feel the way to weight your ski, even with your heel up. Once you are comfortable with this, do some traverses switching lead skis without letting either of those heels touch the ski and while keeping the weight over both skis. You are learning to keep both those feet weighted and underneath you. Keep at it—you're building some good muscle memory.

Once you feel good about traversing, you're ready for the next step. Make some linked turns with both those heels up off your skis, and be prepared to look positively ridiculous—the tip-toe motions will be a goofy dance that would make Pee-Wee Herman envious. If you are keeping both feet weighted and underneath you, this should feel easy. If not, keep practicing 'til the police come and haul you off.

30 Hacky Sack on skis

This tip is meant to really test your ability to use that uphill (back) ski and pressure it with your boot. Ski along in a smooth traverse on a mellow slope, and hold your best tele-stance. Imagine you have a Hacky Sack on your downhill (front) knee, and try to bounce it up in the air. This means lifting the front ski *up and off the snow*, just for an instant. Make sure that back heel stays off your ski while bouncing the Hacky Sack. It's harder than you think, and it takes some concentration. You'll only manage this if you're really weighting that back ski with a nicely pressured boot. See how smooth you can get, as you traverse and repeatedly bounce that little sack on your knee.

31 Hold a beach ball

The shape of your upper body is essential to good ski technique. Remember, your torso and your feet are connected. Creating a nice strong position from your hips up will maximize control of your skis.

Here's a good visual tool to create a strong stance: Think about holding a huge beach ball, or better yet, one of those giant bouncy-ball desk chairs. (Some tele-theorists will tell you to do a full-body pantomime of a satellite dish for the same rounded effect.) Glom onto this enormous ball as you face down the hill. You want a nice *rounded* shape, from your knees, to your hips, and all the way up to your nose. Hold the ball with your hands out in front of you, so you're ready for anything. If some big bully kicks sand in your face and tries to steal your beach ball, you just cradle it that much closer as you knock him down

Without the
BALL
yer poze can get
TOO ANGULAR!

and continue to cruise down the slope.

The gigantic ball shape keeps you from bending too sharply at your waist. And it helps correct the opposite mistake too, when you strut along in the supermodel stance with your shoulders too far back. This isn't a fashion runway, this is powerhouse tele-skiing!

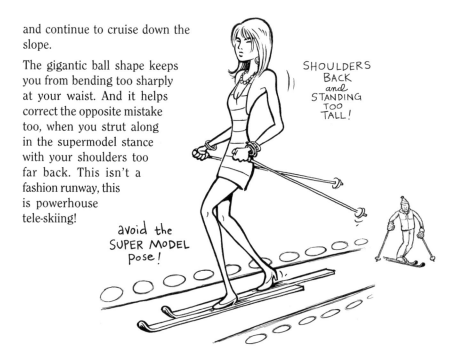

SHOULDERS
BACK
and
STANDING
TOO
TALL!

avoid the
SUPER MODEL
pose!

32 Bungee between the feet

Getting too spread out? Need to keep those feet closer together? Try this trick: Take a short length of thin bungee cord and tie it between your boots. Make it snug enough so you can separate your feet the amount necessary for a tidy stance—just a little longer than one boot length is plenty. Let that bungee pull those feet together. They resist spreading out and instead work in harmony as you move turn to turn. For obvious reasons, don't ski a double black diamond with a little stretchy string tying your boots together. This is bunny-hill-only stuff.

Another way to practice this is to tie your knees together with an appropriate snugness.

BOING!

33 Retraction

Visualize your legs as the landing gear on a big mechanical contraption, and you have the ability to pull a lever in the cockpit and retract these legs up into your fuselage. We can mimic this same mechanism. Just imagine that you are bringing your legs *up toward your body* in each turn. This is the opposite of getting scrunched down toward the snow—it's a mindset of smoothly retracting the landing gear upward.

Obviously, as you zip over the snow, it's your legs that are going to contend with any irregularities. The legs are your shock absorbers, responding to every bump, protuberance, and mogul. But don't let your upper body get low; instead, concentrate on your legs coming up.

With free-heel bindings, the tele-position is an excellent stance for absorbing any clump or inconsistency in the snow, since it provides both front and back stability. So as you bash through lumpy snow, let the landing gear do all the work and keep a quiet upper body.

THE
FALL
LINE!

34 A flashlight in your belly button

Beautiful telemarkers will constantly keep their upper body facing down the fall line. This is a skiing fundamental. Think of your belly button as a flashlight that you must keep pointed directly down the hill. As you ski, keep that beam on something straight down the slope, and don't let it waver! This mental image works wonderfully because it forces you to point your hips down the fall line.

By rotating your hips you can DIRECT the Beam!

The Fall Line   **37**

VVRRRR!

THE FALL LINE

35 Get sucked down the fall line

Imagine you have a long piece of string protruding from your belly button. The other end is stuck in a giant vacuum cleaner down the slope, straight in the fall line. The instant you push off for your run, the vacuum gets turned on, and you get sucked down the fall line. That string (gravity) wants to pull you directly down the hill. Don't fight it! If you get out of the fall line or hold a turn too long, the string will get stressed out and torque you off balance. Don't let that happen—submit yourself fully to the fall line. Embrace gravity!

36 Focus on something downhill

When you drive down the highway, are you focused on the pavement directly below your grille? No! You want to drink in the big picture and focus on that vanishing point way up ahead. Same with skiing. Pick something downslope to focus on. It can be anything: a tree, a lump of snow, or your partner. Make sure it is directly down the fall line, and ski toward it. Keep more than your eyes on it—focus your entire upper body on it. Think about hugging it. Of course, it's advised you pick another object to focus on once you start getting close, especially if it's a tree. Collisions are not recommended.

37 Picture frames

Want a quick way to insure you're facing down the hill while you ski? Hold your poles up in front of you and *frame* something directly down the fall line. Now ski downhill, keeping that object in the frame you created. If you rotate your upper body (even a little), you'll have a hard time keeping it framed. Practice skiing this way to get yourself accustomed to facing straight down the hill. Make a mental image of how it looks and feels with your frame—it should feel the same when you go back to using your poles in their normal configuration.

38 Side-slip in a corridor

This exercise has a three-part progression, from beginner to intermediate to expert.

Here's the first part, for **beginners.** Find a mellow slope with a smooth surface. Visualize a nice corridor that runs downhill, right in the fall line. This "hallway" is just a little wider than the length of your skis. While in the tele-stance, practice *side-slipping* down the fall line. Hold an edge then release it, then slip down and hold the edge again. Keep your skis perpendicular to the fall line. Stay inside your corridor; don't let yourself slide forward (or back) but just slide smoothly straight down the fall line. Make sure you are weighting the uphill ski during this exercise. This will help instill that sweet spot where you are in balance over both skis. It will drive home the fundamentals of a good stance—holding the ball, pressuring the tongues of your boots, and putting weight on the ball of your foot.

Part two is an **intermediate** tip. Use the same slope and same corridor. Now, in the tele-stance, begin the same smooth side-slip downhill. But, add a *transition* and the *opposite tele-pose*, all while staying in that narrow corridor! It's tricky, no? The shuffling motion requires an extra bit of concentration, especially that opposite tele-position. This will depend on skillfully releasing your edges throughout the entire range of the tele-shuffle.

The grand finale is for the **expert.** Do nice, slow *telemark turns* while in that same narrow corridor. This means buttery smooth motions, going straight down the fall line. Can you make a turn without going any wider than the lengths of your skis? The only way to accomplish this graceful trick is to efficiently release those edges, and let the skis slide nice and smooth. For best results, attempt this on a well-groomed bunny slope.

39 Pivot slip

Are you "throwing" your downhill ski forward too fast? Do you need more smoothness in your turning? Practice skiing with a bowlegged cowboy stance (see tip 53), but keep your *tips* spaced just slightly wider than your *tails*. To initiate your turn in this pose, focus on your downhill knee and allow it to roll outward. You'll immediately feel the edge release as the base of your ski rides flatter on the snow. This ski will seek the fall line, and you'll start your turn.

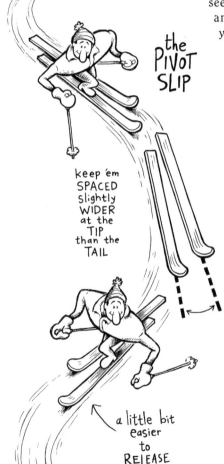

the **PIVOT SLIP**

keep 'em SPACED slightly WIDER at the TIP than the TAIL

a little bit easier to RELEASE EDGES

SMOOTH initiation

SHIFT WEIGHT

ROLL the DOWNHILL KNEE OUTWARD

SKIS SLIGHTLY WIDER at the TIP

EDGE RELEASE and a FLATTER SKI

SMOOTH TURN

Think of your front knee as being connected to your chin: As you roll that knee outward, your chin follows and you shift your upper-body weight in the direction of the turn. Tele-logicians call this a pivot slip.

Cultivate this wide-tip stance on the bunny slope, and feel how smooth the turns and transitions become. Every motion should be slow and progressive—keep consistent pressure on both skis, minimize any up and down, and no quick movements. Practice with this pose, and work your way into steeper terrain. It works like magic in bumps and cruddy snow.

Want an extra challenge? Use this wide-tip stance and go through all three steps in tip 38.

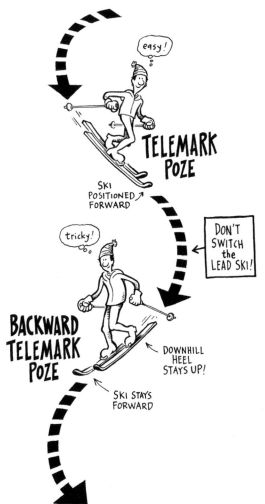

④⓪ The mono-mark

The *mono-mark* is a much-loved specialty turn. Here's a drill that's a great way to find that sweet spot above your skis.

Pick a side to do a tele-turn—let's say right foot forward—for one arcing left turn. After that, *don't switch leads* going into the next turn. Just keep that right foot forward and do a tele-turn to the right, keeping that left heel up and off the ski. One side will feel weird because it's kind of backward, but just keep linking turns without any transition. Practice making turns seamlessly while keeping the same lead ski, and work at it until it feels nice and smooth.

This simple trick forces you to do two things: release those edges and pressure that back foot. It won't work if you are in the backseat, so be sure to keep pressure on the shin of the front boot. After you have mastered one lead ski, switch and work on the other.

41 Smear peanut butter

This tip is essential if you're sporting big side-cut skis. No longer do we weight and un-weight our skis as dramatically as in the bygone era of the Walkman. Now, in the iPod age, we pressure our skis throughout the entire turn, adding more pressure as we complete the turn, then letting off *only a little* as we transition to the next turn. Once we switch lead skis, we begin to add pressure into the next turn.

Imagine a thick layer of peanut butter spread across the entire base of each ski, tip to tail. Think about smearing peanut butter off the bottom as you ski. That stuff is thick and sticky, so don't be timid about really pushing down. Spread it out with the entire length of your skis, nice and consistent through the turn *and* the transition. It's not easy at first, but concentrate on keeping pressure right through the slow transition. Or, imagine skiing across a giant piece of bread spread all over with a thick layer of peanut butter.

This isn't the time for chunky—think smooth!

42 Ski inside the tunnel

Imagine you are skiing in a tube-shaped tunnel—everything is nice and smooth, and it's curving down the slope. Each graceful bend exactly matches your turns. It's just low enough that you can hold the tele-pose, but you can't quite stand up straight or your head will slide against the top. No bobbing up and down; instead, keep your knees bent as you switch leads and *pressure both skis* into the next turn. Think about your skis sliding up, just a little bit, along the inside of the circular tube. Feel those skis efficiently *carve* in the turn instead of skidding.

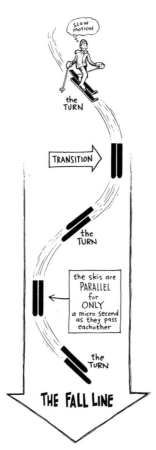

㊸ Slow-motion turns

The act of linking tele-turns can be practiced in slow motion as one smooth continual movement, not a series of disjointed steps. Keep your feet consistently moving in a calm, deliberate pace. Think *slow motion*. Focus on one fluid movement that takes the entire length of the turn. Keep everything steady, nothing herky-jerky.

For this exercise, make sure to move slowly and deliberately during the lead change. This might feel challenging, so concentrate on actively releasing your edges and calmly gliding through the transition on your bases. The time it takes to make the lead change should be the same as that of the turn. Concentrate on a consistent shuffle, with no hesitation or stalling, always gliding at the same speed—don't allow yourself to speed up as you come out of your turn and ease into the fall line. Start with big turns and make yourself take a lot of time. Next, begin to shorten the radius of each turn. Don't hold your edges during the shorter turns, and don't snap through the transition.

This is more than just a slow-motion practice drill—it's a statement of good technique, confident and comfortable. Take it with you beyond this practice session and into your tele-skiing.

PRESSURE   (!)   BOING!

CARVING   HALFWAY   UN·WEIGHTING

44 Spectrum of weighting and un-weighting

Master skiers aren't confined to just one style; instead, they are constantly adjusting their skiing technique to changing conditions and diverse terrain. Sometimes the territory will require carving out giant slalom turns, while other zones might call for snappy bouncing turns.

Don't make the mistake of getting stuck in just one technique. The terrain and snow should dictate your style. It might be crucial in some conditions to keep those skis in full contact with the snow, but other times you'll want to be dramatically weighting and un-weighting. When the snow is absolute manky mush, experts jump their skis up out of the snow to get them to turn.

Imagine a continuum with cute, bouncy bunny (un-weighting) turns on one end and smooth, steady (pressuring) turns on the other. You should be able to place yourself anywhere on that line and perform magic. Practice different styles, and strive to master 'em all.

45 Know the pros and cons of getting low and standing tall

There is no right or wrong here: It's all skiing, and you can make beautiful turns either way. Both these skiers are in the exact same point in their turn, but one is demonstrating the low style while the other is standing tall. Each of these styles has its place. A versatile skier will be strong in both positions because there are places and snow conditions that favor each mode. Once upon a time, the tele-turn required the low stance because the gear was so light and dainty, the only way to achieve stability was to keep the center of gravity low. But today you get a lot more security with big, bold gear, which means you can keep your body up higher.

Getting low (old-school style):

- Very stable
- Short poles de rigueur
- Lotta work on a long day
- Closer to the snow if you fall
- Knees more exposed in a fall
- Easier to get face shots
- Looks really cool (at least Mike! thinks so)
- Performs well in crud and on the steeps
- Easier to regain balance
- Humongous GS turns

Standing tall (the modern look):

- Quicker and easier transition from turn to turn
- Plastic boots favor this stance
- Hard to ski under low branches
- Higher center of gravity
- Easier on the knees
- More spring in your legs to absorb bumps
- Performs well on groomers, corn, and powder
- Easier to release edges
- Lots of room to "bottom out"

46 The "C" stance

By facing down the hill and really reaching for it with your upper body, you create more torque to help bring your skis around. You should feel your body make the shape of the letter *C*. This arcing shape begins with your toes and follows right up through your head. If you stand upright (like the letter *I*), it becomes harder to twist your hips so they face downhill. The steeper the slope, the greater "C" stance you want. No need to arc as aggressively on a mellow slope—just a humble parenthesis will do.

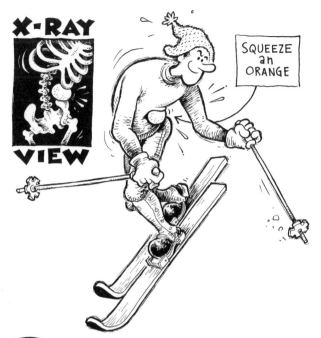

47 Squeeze an orange between your hip and rib cage

You can get a good feel for the arcing "C" stance by imagining squeezing an orange between your hip and ribs. As you alternate between each turn, think about really gripping that orange. This creates a dramatic curve in your body.

Another way to think about this full-body curve is to imagine the uphill side of your torso as *longer* and the downhill side as *shorter*.

PRETTY GOOD
STANCE...

BEND FORWARD

AWESOME
STANCE!

48 Bend at that hip

You can squeeze even more power out of your "C" stance by aggressively bending forward from the hip. This extra forward lean creates a superpowerful body position that can bring those skis around with even more snap. It also keeps you weighted over your skis, engaging them into the snow. It should feel like your upper body is gracefully falling down the hill as you make each turn. The *steeper* the slope, the *more you bend*. Bending at the hip allows your upper body to lead the way.

49 Lead with your chin

When you lean your body downhill, don't lead with your nose—that forces you to look at your ski tips. Lead with your chin—this forces you to look downhill. Imagine a graceful arc from your feet, up your body, and out through your chin. Go ahead and dramatically jut your chin out; it actually lines your entire body up in a strong and powerful stance. It really works! With poor chin technique, every part of your body position suffers.

🌑50 Practice the body position

This simple exercise helps you recognize (and feel) the proper body position for tele-turns. Have a friend stand below you in the fall line—a big friend works great in this role. Each of you holds onto your poles, and your pal leans back and pulls. Maintain the tele-position across the fall line, and fight that pull. C'mon, really tug! You need to work against the downhill tugging, and when you do, you'll score a bunch of excellent style points. It's a natural instinct to set yourself up in a perfect telemark stance. The "C" shape, hands out front, big toe little toe, and a nice tight stance all come into play. Practice in each direction, and work on creating some impeccable muscle memory.

51 Quiet upper body

Ever watch those gnarly ski videos of rad dudes skiing impossibly steep snowfields? Take note of their upper-body position. You'll see that their skis are aggressively pounding through the snow, but from the waist up, they're composed and tranquil. This independent motion, between the legs and the torso, allows for a graceful transition from one turn to the next. The upper body is anticipating each turn, and the legs do the hard work.

52 Uphill hand over the downhill ski

While you may be keeping both those hands in your field of view (see tip 93), the next question to ask yourself is whether or not that hand is reaching far enough to be over your downhill ski. This is a tidy way to focus on your *hand,* and it automatically pulls your shoulder over, creating good upper body posture. This is especially helpful in steeper terrain.

If your hand isn't over that ski, then no wonder you've been having a hard time making those steep turns!

53 Cowboy stance

With big fat skis, we need a big fat stance. If you ski with your feet too close together, you can't take full advantage of the power of those fat skis. For this tip, let's widen that stance out by riding a horse—a really big one! Keep your boots about shoulder width apart. The benefit of practicing with the extra-wide *cowboy stance* is an independent two-footedness, so you can smoothly release the edge of the front ski just a little earlier. Plus, you get some extra balance and it allows you to weight that back ski more aggressively.

54 The balloon squeeze

Looking for that perfect stance? Then stick a balloon between your legs—not a big weather balloon, but one of those nice round balloons that clowns hand out to kids. If your stance is too wide, the balloon will keep falling out, so tighten up to keep it in place. For those alpine skiers who just can't seem to stick with the tele-stance through the turn, the balloon will help keep those legs apart so you can't cheat by slipping in a quick parallel stance.

Skiing with a balloon between your legs is tricky because it's round and slippery against nylon pants. After practicing a while with the real thing, all you will need to do is imagine holding something between your legs. This exercise forces you to keep your legs together as you ski.

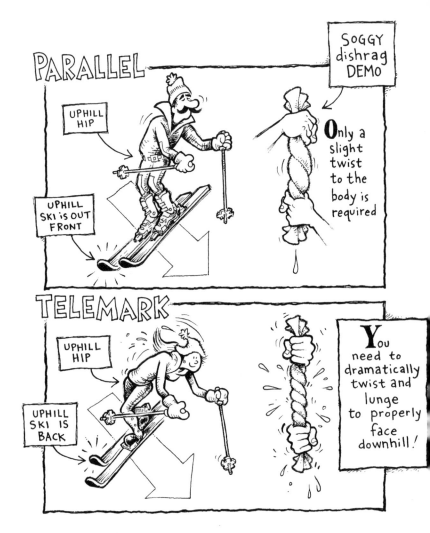

55 Parallel vs. tele-twist

This book talks a lot about twisting your upper body so you face downhill. Our parallel-turning comrades need to twist too, but not quite as much as we do. The reason is the different positions of our uphill skis. The parallel skier has the *uphill ski forward,* which transfers to the uphill hip, causing it to face down the fall line with minimal twisting.

In the telemark turn, the *uphill ski is back*. This forces the hip up into the hill, but you want to keep that hip facing down the fall line. To solve this, you need to dramatically *twist* and *lunge* to correctly get yourself facing downhill. Think of your torso as a wet dishrag and you're twisting to get all that water out. No matter how you ski, parallel or telemark, you always want to have those hips aimed down the fall line.

56 The windup

Telemark skiing requires some extra twisting compared to an alpine turn (see the previous tip). Finish each turn by twisting your spine like a spring so your upper body is facing down the hill into the next turn. The action of your skis crossing the fall line will wind the spring up nice and tight. There is a lot of power in this coiled-up stance because it sets you up to initiate your next turn.

Practice by exaggerating the twisting to the point that it gets uncomfortable, then *explode* into the next turn! Let the energy and rebound from the spring do the work, and simply allow your skis to make quick transitions from side to side. A strong rhythm is crucial.

57 Use short poles

You want those hands in front of you, not above your head somewhere. If you are making your turns from a low stance, you want short poles. This makes it easier to keep your hands in front of you. Some beginning tele-skiers find this tip super-helpful, and they benefit from some time with ridiculously tiny poles, as it forces a solid stance.

Skiing with alpine-length poles is great as long as you have a nice tall stance. But long poles and a short stance just don't work, and you end up in that classic "Praise the Lord" pose from a bygone era of tele-skiing. Shorten your adjustable-probe poles, or steal a pair from a five-year-old.

The GENERAL RULES of POLE HEIGHTS

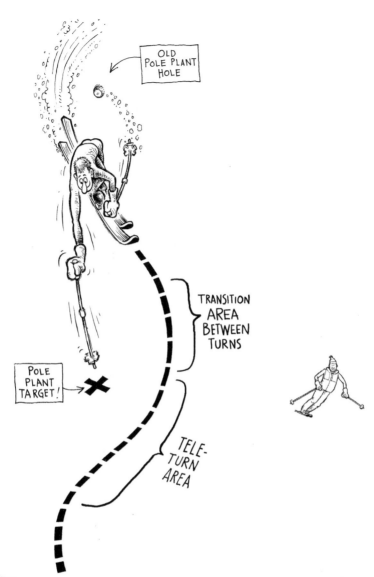

OLD
POLE PLANT
HOLE

TRANSITION
AREA
BETWEEN
TURNS

POLE
PLANT
TARGET!

TELE-
TURN
AREA

58 Reach downhill

The act of reaching aggressively downhill with each pole plant has multiple benefits. For one thing, it sets you up for the next turn because it keeps your upper body positioned in the fall line. This puts you in a great position to make quick turns using just your lower body. Second, *reaching downhill* keeps you *leaning downhill*. It doesn't allow that timid pose where your torso tilts uphill into the slope. By concentrating on downhill pole plants, you can break the bad habit of uphill pole plants. Third, reaching aggressively downhill will keep both hands out in front of you, creating the athletic stance of the expert tele-skier.

the BASKET
comes around
in sync
with the turn

REACH!

NEXT
POLE
PLANT
TARGET!

59 Timing downhill pole plants

To keep yourself in the fall line, you need to make each and every pole plant downhill. Timing is crucial. You swing your pole downhill when you're at the lowest point of your compression; this initiates the next turn. Then *plant* just as you *rise up* out of your turn. The hand that has just planted the pole should stay out in front of your body, to point down the fall line. Don't let it get behind you.

A nice image is to picture a string connecting the basket of your pole to your hip. As you swing, the string pulls you forward. This swinging motion can help pull you forward to begin releasing those edges.

SINK DOWN
into
POLE PLANT

Just
quickly
"STING"
the snow

60 Turn around the pole plant

After you plant your pole, ski around it and set up for the next pole plant. Don't ever let your pole linger in the snow—just quickly sting the slope, and as you turn around it, snap it out. You should already be set up for the next pole plant and reaching downhill. Don't lean on a pole after it's planted; it's not there for support, it's just a tool for timing. Also, your uphill hand (or shoulder) shouldn't linger anywhere behind you. Keep both hands in front, and keep reaching forward.

If you need a nice staccato mantra, try this: *Plant-Turn! Plant-Turn!* Then work up to a more powerful *Plant-Punch! Plant-Punch!*

61 Punch downhill with that uphill hand

This is an aggressive way to get your uphill hand back in front of you after each pole plant: The classic pose of the heavyweight boxer is the perfect attitude. Just imagine socking someone shorter than you down the fall line. Don't hold back—you can forcefully lead with your shoulder to get some KO power. Also, having your hands down the hill keeps you from sagging into the slope behind you. It directs your torso downward and not back into the slope. Keeping those hands out in front assures that your upper body is rotated down the fall line and in a good balanced position, and you'll always be ready for that next pole plant.

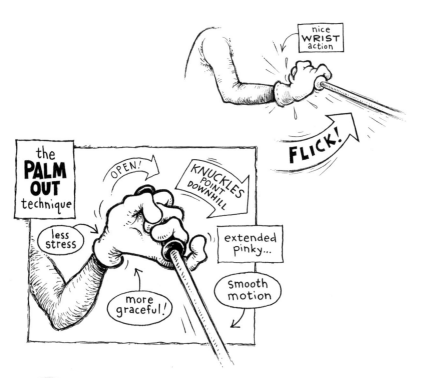

62 Use your wrist

For a nice, quick pole plant, flick the pole up in front of you with your wrist. Reach out with your pole, then plant it and go. Keep your knuckles pointing downhill. This isn't a big motion—imagine being in a sports car and shifting into third gear.

You can also think about keeping your palm facing out just a little. This will help open your body up to the fall line, and it actually gives you a little more reach with each pole plant. Imagine peeking through a curtain with each turn, using your downhill hand to open it up just enough to sneak through.

63 Tossing a pole

If you've lost one of your poles, you can still get down the hill just fine. You'll need to toss your pole from hand to hand as you make turns. Don't just pass it between your hands, actually toss it! The rhythm is: *Plant, turn, toss! Plant, turn, toss!* No need to buy a new pole—tossing one will keep you facing directly downhill.

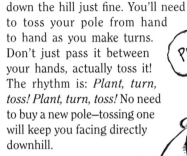

PLANT, TURN, TOSS!

64 Double pole plants on the downhill side

You really want to get tricky? Try doing double pole plants. But not the tried-and-true double-poling you might remember from the bygone days of leather boots and bamboo poles. No, in this double pole plant you are planting *both* poles on the *downhill* side of your skis. This forces you to rotate your upper body over your skis (otherwise, it's almost impossible to do), and it keeps your hands in a strong downhill position. Yes, it's kooky looking, but it forces you to aggressively correct some awkward habits.

65 Breathe

This may sound ridiculous, but when your mind is swamped with dozens of little tricks, you can actually forget to breathe. It's hard to link a bunch of turns together if your brain is oxygen starved. If you are forgetting to breathe (and this is surprisingly common), simply tell yourself to *take a big breath with each turn*. Don't be afraid to huff and puff out loud. Besides being good practice for natural childbirth, it will help define a nice rhythm.

66 Stay relaxed

Any skier who's free of tension can make it all look easy. If you're all uptight, you simply can't do the important stuff to achieve good style. If you can eliminate stress from your psyche, your profound vital-force will thrive. You will be at one with the universe. Picture the world as yours and it will be. Relax, calm down, loosen up, don't worry, let it come to you; you are the master of the all-important, penultimate tele-turn. Your muscle memory will spring into action, and the magic of the telemark turn will take over.

Remember To . . .

67 Enjoy the skin back up

If you want to stray away from the lifts, slapping on the skins and sliding uphill is a necessity. You don't see many pictures in magazines featuring the skin track, but it's an integral part of backcountry skiing. If you can learn to embrace the up-track, you'll be a happy skier. The joys of off-piste travel are enormous: It's out in the beautiful mountains (versus behind a desk), and your lungs are filled with clean air. If the backcountry is a new experience, don't get frustrated because you have to slog uphill—there are plenty of benefits to earning your turns. God gave you your very own high-speed quads, so enjoy using them.

WIPE OUT your EYEWEAR

BLOW SNOT

DRINK!

Think POSITIVE thoughts

Be mindful of your CHI

cinch down and POWDER PROOF your clothes

snug up your COMPRESSION STRAPS

EAT!

make tinkle

Shorten your POLES!

remove HEEL LIFTS

TIGHTEN your BOOTS

SCRAPE the SNOW off your WAX POCKET

PEEL SKINS

68 Before your turn

Don't just peel 'em and squeal 'em! When you are skinning (or booting) in the backcountry, take a few minutes to collect yourself after that long uphill hump. You've earned it. Do all the important things before your run to insure success. Enjoy the view, drink some water, center your karma, and then pick out that perfect line and let 'er rip.

⟨69⟩ Know when to call it a day

Feeling the burn? If you're skiing lousy at the end of a long day, don't add exhaustion to your list of problems. Go home (and study this book!) before you need to call a knee surgeon.

70 Get Allen and Mike's other book!

The skills needed for backcountry skiing go way beyond the humble telemark turn. We worked hard to fill *Allen & Mike's Really Cool Backcountry Ski Book* with all the info you will ever need for camping and traveling in the winter. Maybe this tip seems like shameless self-promotion (in fact, it is), but these two books are designed to complement each other. Part of the joy of tele-skis is the fact you can use them in the backcountry.

We know you will be better prepared with these books on your shelf, or better yet, in your backpack!

71 Find a mantra

Relax and breathe is a good mantra and it really works! Say it before you push off downhill and repeat it with each turn. The advantage of a mantra is that it helps set a rhythm for nice even turns. *Smooth turns, embrace gravity,* or *face downhill* are all good mantras. Thinking about your pole plants can help. Whatever you use, keep it simple and pick one thing to focus on for each run. Don't swamp your mind with every tip in the book. If you do that, nothing will work. A little positive energy goes a long way, so visualize success.

72 Keep the parallel turn in your bag of tricks

Parallel turns in a telemark book? Well, if you already know how to ski in an alpine stance, don't assume you will never use this turn on free-heel skis. It's totally worth knowing how to telemark *and* parallel because the two turns complement each other. If you have a lifetime of alpine skiing and the tele-turn is a new thing for you, the parallel turn is a great position to fall back on when things get out of hand. Sometimes gloppy snow conditions and tight trees might get a long-dormant alpine skier to reemerge out of necessity.

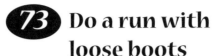

73 Do a run with loose boots

Dare yourself to give this tip a try. Bend down and completely unbuckle everything from the knees down. No cheating allowed. You'll need to perfectly center yourself over your skis. This tip demands that you discover the secret *sweet spot* over your skis, the subtle spot where you want to be skiing all the time. You might never find this delicate point of balance with your boots cranked down tight.

Want an extra challenge? Find a pair of smelly old leather boots at a garage sale and try them on the slopes. These limp boots require extra finesse, which will transfer directly to more style. And, you'll reap the benefits when the big plastics go back on.

74 Spoon the tracks of a better skier

This is an especially good tip if you are trying to figure out how to make the same beautiful tracks as those of the skier you envy. It helps push you to learn a new style of skiing and to make a cleaner line, and it may help you develop that rhythm you have been missing. Plus, you'll sleep better at night knowing you've embraced this guilt-free technique of eco-groovy powder conservation.

Spoonin'

spoon·ing \ˈspün-in\ *vt*, **1:** as stacked spoons in the silverware drawer **2:** to preserve powder using righteous track hugging technique \ *adj* spoon·ey; -est **3:** powder farming, similar to 8's. **example:** *"Let's skin back up and I'll spoon your tracks!"*

75 Review your tracks

Skiing gracefully is an expressive art form. The tracks you create are really works of creativity that can tell you a lot about your skiing. Here's what to look for:

- **Are the pole plants on the inside of the turns?** Downhill pole plants should be.

- **Are the turns even?** If you have a "bad" side, those turns are usually bigger.

- **Are you hesitating somewhere in your turn?** You'll see a traversing track.

- **Are the transitions smooth?** If they're too fast, they'll look Z-shaped.

- **Are the tracks too straight?** Round them out and finish each turn.

- **Are you dragging your poles?** If so, each turn will have a stripe next to it.

- **Are you carving nice "railroad" grooves?** This is especially easy to see in the corduroy.

76 Ski without your poles

Going without your poles helps improve your balance and gives you one less thing to think about. Concentrate on facing down the hill with your upper body. Too many skiers depend on their poles as an extra point of balance. This exercise is a real eye opener because you are unable to cheat—you are forced into a balanced stance. You can also hold your poles like a kayak paddle. Pretend you are delivering a tray of fine wine to your friends down the fall line, and be careful—that stuff is expensive!

Want something more challeng-ing? Simply balance your poles on top of your wrists.

the track is
nice and
SNAPPY!

77 Make short, fast turns

This tip may be all you need if you feel stuck in long, wide turns. Simply making quicker turns might be what it takes to bring it all together. Try it on an easy slope. Work on quick transitions and make each turn short and fast—don't hesitate! The moment you start coming out of one turn, immediately make the transition into the next. Think about aggressively bringing those skis around, especially the tails. Having short-radius turns in your bag of tricks is a necessity for certain snow conditions and for skiing in the trees.

78 Ski the trees

This is an environment where you *need* to turn fast. You'll be surprised at how quickly you can turn when you have no choice—it's common to see intermediate skiers make expert turns in the face of a lodgepole pine. You have to react as you ski, planning only a couple of turns in advance. Be careful, though. Tree skiing isn't the place to push your limits. Don't be ashamed to perform a controlled fall in self-defense. It's far better to land on your butt in snow than on your head in wood.

A tip for skiing the trees: It is important to look at the empty places *between* the trees and focus on where you want to go, not at the trees. We tend to go where we are looking.

⓱ Use a lurk

If you were skiing a hundred years ago in the snowy countryside of Norway, you'd be holding your trusty lurk. What's a lurk? It's the long wooden staff used by the pioneers of the telemark turn. Early in the twentieth century someone got the idea of using two poles, one in each hand. However, the single-pole technique of yore has some advantages when you're learning to turn because you hold it with both hands. This forces you to fully rotate and keep your hands out in front of you, which in turn keeps your weight over your skis.

Try this exercise: Hold your lurk out in front of you like a kayak paddle and try to tap the snow with the end on the downhill side. Actually, you may choose to drag the tip, and that's good form too. Instead of mail-ordering a real lurk from Norway, simply try extending your probe poles out to a nice long length.

⟨80⟩ Find your rhythm

Skiing is a dynamic sport that demands rhythm. For some of us, this rhythm comes from the cadence of each pole plant. For others, it's the up and down or the back and forth. Breathing out loud with each turn is another great way to develop a rhythm. Sing to yourself. Find something that gives you a feel for doing nice even turns. Discover your own rhythm, with or without an MP3 player.

SWEEP into NEXT TURN

81 Headlights on the knees

Imagine you have a pair of headlights on your knees, and you point the beam in the direction of your turn as if you are steering a car. Bent knees are nice and pointy, and the *arrow* they create is directed into each turn. However, your headlights only stay attached to bent knees—if you stand up and straighten your leg, the lamp will pop off. So keep your knees bent and *shining into* each turn. If this is too much to think about, concentrate only on your back knee. Make the light from this knee sweep around smoothly into each turn.

the track
from
HOCKEY STOP
turns will be more
"Z"
shaped...

SNAP!

82 Hockey stops

Think of those quick stops that hockey players make, spraying ice up into the camera lens. Do that same quick twist and weighting of the skis with each of your turns. This slows you down and forces the camber out of the skis. As the skis rebound at the end of the turn, use this energy to your advantage by un-weighting and initiating the next turn. It should feel as though you are springing off your boards and snapping into the next turn.

Sometimes an overemphasized hockey-stop turn will result in an exaggerated windshield-wiper effect. The problem is that you dump speed so efficiently, you almost come to a complete halt, and this produces unwanted Z-shaped tracks. Fortunately, this is an easy problem to correct: Just lessen the power of that snap-twist and allow your turns to melt smoothly into each other.

TIGHTENING
and
UNSCREWING

ORGANIC
PEANUT
BUTTER

83 Unscrew a jar lid

Imagine holding a large jar between your knees. As you switch lead skis, you alternate between screwing the lid off and on. Feel the lid as it rotates, and put some squeezing pressure on it so you don't drop the jar. This helps tighten up your stance and gives a good visual image of how your knees should pass by each other during your transition between turns. If you have big fat skis, which require a wider stance, just visualize an extra-large peanut butter jar.

84 Sneaking

A simple way to collect yourself into a nice tight tele-stance is to *sneak* your way down the slope. It's impossible to get too spread out and wobbly if you're sneaking. Go ahead and pantomime that classic, scrunched-down, cartoonish body language. Do your best to quietly tiptoe down the slopes.

SHHH!

first:
Gently hold
a PENNY between
your butt cheeks

85 Squeeze those butt cheeks

It's every tele-skier's dream to tighten up their stance, but sometimes those feet just get too far apart. To fix this, take a penny (or at least pretend to) and carefully place it between your butt cheeks. Next, squeeze those butt cheeks together and start skiing. C'mon, really work those muscles! Concentrate on not letting go of that penny. You'll realize instantly that you simply can't let those legs get spread out. As you make each turn, don't let up on the Gluteus Maximus Grip.

next:
Squeeze those
BUTT CHEEKS together
while skiing
and
DON'T LET GO OF
THAT PENNY!

86 Bending modestly

Women have a powerful advantage when perfecting their telemark stance. Trying to retain some degree of modesty while bending down with a miniskirt on has created an opportunity to practice exactly the balanced stance you need for tele-turns. So if you are a guy and are having some trouble with the stance, try slipping on something short and tight and have a friend review your technique. Practice makes perfect!

YIN
the Transition
(UN-WEIGHTING)

YANG
the TURN!
(WEIGHTING)

⟨87⟩ Mystical truths revealed within the telemark turn

Look beyond the earthly limitations of the telemark turn. The duality of existence can be seen in the humble telemark skier. In the transition between turns (un-weighting), the skier is reaching and expanding upward toward the heavens like a lotus flower in spring, floating beyond the limitations of gravity and heavy snow. This action is the *yin*. In the turn (weighting), everything is reversed. Power and force contract into the dynamic warrior. Going beyond merely pressuring a turn, the warrior attacks it like a samurai in battle. This is the *yang*.

The mystical truth is that the yin and the yang are eternally linked. One cannot exist without the other. This is the insight into the beauty of telemark skiing. You are both yin and yang; the transition and the turn flow into one. The un-weighting gives way to the weighting and around it goes. It's cosmic.

HARD PACK
2 Dimensional skiin[g]
(Yawn...)

Working them EDGES

88 Hard pack vs. powder

These are as different as New Hampshire and Utah. Hard pack (found at ski areas, although corn snow in the backcountry is hard pack too) exists on a two-dimensional plane. The surface is something you stay on top of. Your turns are done by biting in with your edges, and it hurts when you fall.

Powder is another world. You are moving through a three-dimensional volume of puffy wonderfulness, side to side and up and down within the snow. It's a joyous experience that mimics flying—no wonder so many of us are addicted. Edges serve little purpose here; instead, you want to ride on your bases and pilot them as a lone platform. Relax and bounce; bob up and down within the snow. The wider and softer the ski, the better. Float on those big boards.

Many an area skier has become discombobulated when confronted with champagne fluff for the first time. Sadly, they're trapped in a two-dimensional mindset. They need to profoundly expand their limited comprehension into the mystical third dimension.

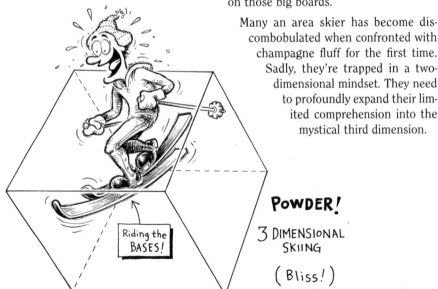

Riding the BASES!

POWDER!

3 DIMENSIONAL SKIING

(Bliss!)

89 Slow-motion bounce!

Skiing powder is as much an attitude as a skill. The one trick that brings it all together is the slow-motion bounce! A cartoon of a bouncing bunny played at half speed is exactly the mindset you want for bottomless fluff, especially with soft, wide skis. This may sound overly simplistic, but let the skis do the work. As you ski, ignore your edges and ride your bases. Find a bounce that matches the shape of your skis. Don't try to fit the skis to a rhythm—instead, let the rhythm fit the skis! It's controlled momentum. Here's a list of tips that work miracles when skiing powder:

- Relax.
- Keep a quiet upper body.
- Weight and un-weight, smoothly and consistently.
- Use the skis' rebound.
- Ski the fall line.
- Pretend you're on one big ski.
- Don't be afraid of a little speed.
- Maintain a tall stance.
- Don't let the skis get sideways to the hill.

It's hard to argue with any of these basics, but they are especially important in deep powder.

⚫**90** **Riding porpoises**

Powder skiing is joyous. Think what it would be like to ride on the back of a porpoise as it dives in and out of the water. These graceful animals arch back and forth as they rise up and drop back down into the water, enjoying every minute of play. If you were to ride on one's back as you skied down the fall line in deep powder, you would get a feel for how your skis should move underneath you in bottomless fluff–compressing as you settle into each turn and changing leads as you rise back up. With springy skis you can actually launch completely out of the snow when you're un-weighting.

91 One big ski

When skiing in powder snow, erase all thoughts of two separate skis; instead, imagine you have just *one big platform* under your feet. You are exploiting your momentum down the hill to direct this giant platform in the magnet of the ever-loving fall line. It's important to distribute your weight directly under you. Don't let the one big ski get too long and skinny; you want to be floating on a *wide* platform. You have the advantage of being able to move your feet independently of the platform. Let each motion of your body flow into the next using just your one giant ski.

92 Really reach down the hill

On steep terrain, you really need to reach down the hill to keep the weight over your skis. Think about reaching with your pole and leaning your upper body down into the next turn. This simple action can induce a powerful body position for dynamic skiing. The *steeper* the terrain, the more *aggressive* you need to be when stretching downhill for that next pole plant.

93 Keep both hands in your field of view

This is important at all times, but it's essential when skiing steep terrain. If you can't see your hands, it means they must be somewhere behind you. You want your hands to be out in front, helping you face the fall line and moving you downhill. Imagine you are piloting a high-performance jet fighter and you need to keep both hands on the control panel in front of you pointing down the fall line.

If you are doing strong pole plants, the downhill hand won't be a problem. It is usually the pesky hand that just *finished* a pole plant that gets left behind. Think about reaching that hand downhill *across* your body so you can see it.

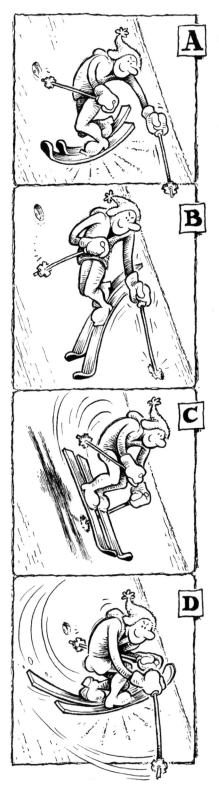

94 Jump turns

There is a time and place for the aggressive jump turn, like manky glop and the steeps. This powerhouse turn requires logging some flight time. For each *transition* you are literally *airborne* as you vault off the snow. You switch leads and direction while in the air and land back on the snow in the opposite turn. Think about down-weighting your skis really hard so they spring back hard, and use the rebound to get up and out of the snow again. While in the air, twist your torso and snap your front foot back—it needs to be behind you in the next tele-pose. Land and compress hard! This is no place for daintiness. Rebound again to start your next turn.

95 Keep your hip away from the slope

Do whatever it takes to keep your uphill hip bone (the iliac crest) as far away as you can from the slope behind you, especially in the steeps. Your hips are the dividing point between your (active) legs and your (quiet) upper body.

A great visual aid is to sandwich your poles around your hips; this will make it easier to comprehend and achieve the masterly body positions. Create distance from your hip and the slope by angling your pelvis down the hill. As you ski, have a partner look at you and tell you if the poles are staying level or if they are leaning into the turn. Don't let them swing around; try to keep them as smooth as a hovercraft. The "plane" the poles create should be tipped a little forward (bending at the hip) and perpendicular to the fall line (twisting at the hip). Once again, this helps create a strong body position that sets you up for releasing your edges.

POLES are ATTACHED using wrist straps LOOPED over the other basket

the poles create a nice visual HIP PLANE

NO TWISTING OR SWINGING

POLES stay smooth on an EVEN PLANE

DON'T DIP YOUR POLES UP the HILL

LAME!

THE FALL LINE

96 Skiing breakable crud

Alas, life isn't just an endless bowl of blower powder. Sometimes you get a spanking. Cruddy conditions are cruddy, true enough. You can't be dainty when the snow is miserable—you have to be aggressive and attack the crud like a 500-pound gorilla. Hunker down low and punch through with each turn. Un-weight aggressively and turn your skis as they leave the snow. Sometimes a primal scream is required.

97 Don't be afraid of a little speed

Airplanes need speed on the runway before they can fly. Are you like an airplane putt-putting down the runway at a miserable crawl? If so, you'll never fly. Those skis need to move before they can blossom into the amazing tools that make skiing so much fun. Don't fight it—let 'em rip! With a little speed they'll float and bounce, and turning them will be easy. Use that momentum to get those skis flying.

98 Whirlybirds

Twin tip skis and the telemark pose open up a whole new realm of grooviness. Most short fat tele-skis have tails that are swooped up for skiing backwards. The first step in trickster-hipness is the Whirlybird; simply put it means twirling around as you ski downhill.

Start on a groomed bunny slope. Make a nice smooth tele-turn (1), but don't swing around into the next turn. Instead, lose a little momentum and let those tips sweep uphill (2) while you let the tails sweep around behind you (3). There's a point where your skis will point directly uphill (4) and you switch leads, but keep the tips moving—and be aware, this feels like it happens fast. The next step requires *super smooth edge release*. Let the tips and tails rotate around like a propeller (5) with YOU being the axis point. As your tips seek the fall line, transition into the turn (6) just like normal and ride downhill. At this point you can go right into another Whirlybird (and a third one), especially if you are in full view of an audience on the chairlift. All this twirling can be done in a corridor (like tip 38) but it'll require masterful edge-release skills. Make that your goal.

When you first attempt the Whirlybird, expect it to be a little awkward. That's okay, just keep at it. Here are a few insights for the beginner: As you sweep your tips uphill (3) allow yourself to almost completely stall out. At that point you'll feel the pull of gravity drag you downhill by your tails; use that pull and just let your tips come around (5) into the fall line. The beginner will do a lot of pole planting as they refine this trick. The perfected Whirlybird is most elegant without pole plants.

99 Backwards skiing

This is the grand finale of the telemark artisan. Let's put those twin tips to work! Once again, it's bunny slope domain. Start off with a Whirlybird, but at the halfway point, let gravity take over and allow yourself to glide into the fallline (1) with the tails pointed downhill.

Look over your *outside* shoulder to see down the slope (2). This pose will help twist your upper body and put the skis in a better position. The transition is tricky with both skis pointing pretty much straight uphill (3). Release your edges and make the turn as smooth as you can, bringing 'em around in a slow curve, and swing your head to look over your other shoulder (4). Don't try to make tight little turns. It's easier to make big rounded arcs (5), especially when looking behind you.

Just so you know, this one was tricky to draw. Mike had to get video footage of Wholesome Ann doing the backwards demo. The funny thing was, that when the video was played backwards, Wh'Ann looked for all the world like she was doing perfect tele-turns—*uphill!*

Tips 100 through 123 are common
Mistakes
(and how to fix 'em!)

💯 Don't get frustrated

Skiing and frustration don't mix. However, this is a very real emotion for folks trying to learn a new skill, especially one as challenging as the telemark turn. When things are not going your way, it's time to stop and regroup. Imagine succeeding with just *one* little aspect of your turn instead of trying to do everything perfectly. Remember that learning is a lifelong process, and it's good for the soul to try something new, if only for the sake of humility. Skiing is fun, and something is wrong if that joy is gone. *See tips 43, 65, 66, 67, 69, 71, and 72.*

(101) Don't freeze into the tele-position

The telemark turn is a dynamic turn. You should always be in motion, either sinking down into the turn or rising up out of it. If you are making really wide turns and long traverses, it means you're stuck in the tele-position too long. It's as if your brain synapses have momentarily stopped firing.

Telemark theorists also call this *shopping for a turn*. It means you are avoiding the inevitable transition into the next turn. You are hanging out when you need to be decisive. Try not to think of each turn as a separate step—they should each melt into the next as one fluid motion. *See tips 22, 23, 35, 36, 43, 71, 74, 77, 80, and 97.*

⬤**102** Too spread out

Yikes! I would hate to fall like this. Being excessively spread out thwarts your ability to properly weight your skis. You lose all the power the beautiful tele-position can deliver. It also keeps you from using your legs as shock absorbers and stalls your momentum for flowing into your next turn. *See tips 26, 32, 42, 45, 54, 77, 82, 83, and 84.*

FRONT LEG is STRAIGHT!

🄚🄞🄣 Bend that front leg

This is a very common mistake. It's imperative to bend both the knee and ankle of your leading leg. This creates a nice tight stance and allows you to absorb whatever the snow surface may throw at you. Have a friend watch you. If you are skiing straight-legged, go back to easier terrain where you can concentrate on skiing in good form. You should be able to feel the pressure of the tongue of your boot against your shin. Work on that muscle memory so you don't need to think about it. *See tips 7, 19, 30, 33, 81, and 86.*

(104) Crossed tips

Imagine a lone ski zooming downhill without any skier attached to it. Visualize how it'll bounce and chatter because it's so light. Any little nuance in the snow will deflect it one way or another. Now, if that ski is clipped into a boot and the boot is on a skier, it's less likely to get deflected, but only if it's weighted! An un-weighted ski will chatter and have a life of its own. When it's the back ski (very common), it'll try to jump over your front ski. When that happens, look out!

The only cure for the ski tips that get all crossed up is to aggressively weight that back ski with good body position and a nice tight stance. *See tips 24, 26, 43, 49, and 53.*

105 Crossed legs

If you are using super-short skis, be aware. Sometimes when you hunker down for that low tele-turn, you stand up and find your legs are crossed! You made two mistakes: First, you got too spread out, enough that your ski tip could sneak behind your other boot. Second, the back ski wasn't weighted enough and wobbled out of its track. To correct this, stand tighter and weight that back ski more. Believe it or not, you can still complete a rather "elegant" wedge-like turn in this pretzel pose. You can even sink into the next turn and actually un-cross your legs with nary a pause in your rhythm. *See tips 27, 45, 53, 54, 83, 84, and 85.*

SKI POSITIONS are WAY TOO EXTREME! looks grim!

THE DREADED

V

SNUGGED UP A LITTLE CLOSER Pretty Good...

YES! AIM FOR THIS!

106 Avoid the Big V

Back in ancient Norway, telemark pioneers skied on wooden skis that were straight, skinny, and long. Very little changed until the mid-1990s, when more dramatic side cut was added to ski design. Early telemakers compensated for this lack of side cut by slightly offsetting the skis in the shape of a V while making turns. This V pattern created a kind of modified side cut and allowed two straight skis to produce a rounded turning surface. For centuries tele-skiers relied on this V shape— it was integral to the tele-turn—but equipment and technique have evolved, and that once beautiful pose has been relegated to old sepia-tinted photographs.

That said, the antiquated V shape is sneaky, and it can still creep into the modern tele-turn. Even an expert skier might sporadically display this obsolete technique. For the novice, it's not a big deal if it's subtle and small. The problem is that sometimes it isn't so subtle. Often the beginning telemarker will display a great big capital V, with the uphill ski in an overly obtuse angle. The back ski then turns into a sluggish outrigger that works against the efficiency of the turn. Instead, you need both skis under you and consistently parallel. The goal is to snap back and forth between turns without any V shape at all. *See tips 7, 26, 32, 33, 41, and 43.*

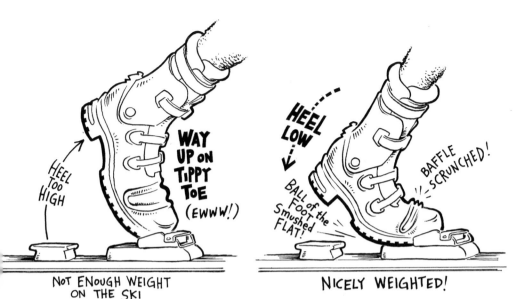

HEEL TOO HIGH

WAY UP ON TIPPY TOE (EWWW!)

NOT ENOUGH WEIGHT ON THE SKI

HEEL LOW

BALL of the Foot the Smushed FLAT!

BAFFLE SCRUNCHED!

NICELY WEIGHTED!

107 Hinging

Hinging is a term that describes a tippy-toe pose with your inside boot. Is your back foot positioned with the heel up high and the toe pointed straight down like a ballet dancer? Without enough weight directed down into the boot, you end up just bending at the toe of your boot versus the baffle. You have no weight on that back foot and thus no control. The outcome is a back ski that gets all squirrelly and trails along behind you instead of under you.

Hinging means the back foot isn't transferring enough weight to the ski. You might have a tippy-toe back foot on a groomer and still feel like you're skiing really well, but that same habit in soft snow (or broken crud) will be disastrous. You need to feel the baffle of your boot adequately scrunched to avoid the dreaded hinging, and this requires deliberate weight on the *ball* of your foot, not the toe! The solution is to *press down* on the ball of that back foot. Imagine a raisin under the ball area—you want that thing to end up paper flat with each turn. *See tips 7, 19, 24, 26, 30, and 41.*

(skidding)

the STRAIGHT "I" STANCE

CH-CHA-CHATTER!

108 Skidding

Are you skidding your turns instead of carving? If your skis are skidding out from underneath you or chattering on the snow, you need to get more weight over them. Or, if the plume of snow coming off your skis is happening at the bottom of your turn rather than at the midway point, you are skidding. Carving requires a fluid motion with constant force applied to your inside edges throughout your turn. *See tips 13, 41, 42, 43, and 44.*

Keeping your upper-body weight over your skis makes them hold well through each arc of the turn. So employ an aggressive "C" stance and bend at your hip to keep your body over your skis, especially the front of your skis. This will create a bold upper-body position, which will transfer right down into the snow. *See tips 46, 48, 49, and 50.*

smooth!

carving!

NICE C SHAPES!

109 Double pole plants

This ancient technique is a holdover from the long-gone days of long poles and leather boots. There are some beautiful skiers who make perfect-looking double pole plants, usually just quick little taps. But, if you depend on double-poling for balance, it's time to work on that single downhill pole plant. The benefits of the alternating pole plant are timing, grace, and good form. Step into the modern era. *See tips 37, 52, 58, 59, 60, 61, 63, and 64.*

110 Don't use your uphill pole as a point of balance

If you find yourself in the all too common habit of uphill pole plants, there is a fundamental flaw to your technique. This is an unmistakable sign that you are somehow out of balance. It means you are leaning *into* the hill, when what you really want is to be leaning *down* the hill and planting that pole down there as well. You don't need that uphill pole for extra balance. Don't be afraid of what's below you. Trust yourself and let your upper body bend downhill. *See tips 22, 35, 36, 37, 57, 63, 71, 74, 76, 77, and 97.*

⬤**111** Spidering

Do you feel like you need lots of extra support from your poles? If so, you need to work on balance while moving downhill on skis. Don't let those poles become a crutch, because they can create some bad habits and inelegant body positions. Spend more time on terrain that isn't intimidating. Put the poles away for a while, and get comfortable schussing along. Focus on good upper-body form. *See tips 11, 31, 37, 57, 63, 76, and 79.*

112 Don't drag your uphill pole

If that pole is hidden somewhere *behind* you, it's like an anchor that keeps you from fully engaging the fall line. This is a common problem, and it'll thwart your initiation into quicker turns. Think about keeping both hands in front of you, and aggressively face yourself downhill. *See tips 37, 57, 59, 60, 61, 63, 76, 92, and 93.*

113 Put your heel lifts down

Once you get to the top of that slope and you peel your skins for the downhill run, don't forget to put your heel lifts down. There is no reason to try to artificially increase the angle of the terrain. Strive for harmony with the slope, and joy and happiness will ensue. If you keep forgetting this fundamental insight, remind yourself with a Post-it note on the inside of your goggles. *See tip 68.*

(114) Unequal weight on the skis

If those skis aren't weighted properly, they'll never behave. Mastery depends on the two skis being weighted perfectly equally. Not enough weight on the back ski, and it'll act all squirrelly. This is all too often the downfall of the alpine skier trying to learn to telemark. Too much weight on the back ski, and you can't control the front ski. This scenario happens in steep terrain when there is a fear of commitment to the fall line. Get that weight over the front ski by reaching down the fall line. *See tips 24, 27, 33, 43, 91, 92, and 95.*

115 Face your body down the hill

This poor guy is riding his skis the way you would push a grocery cart. While he may be looking down the hill with his eyes, his torso and hips are facing across the fall line, just like his skis. Tele-skiing is dynamic and beautiful, not rigid and confining. You want your whole upper body facing down the fall line. The steeper the terrain, the more you twist. *See tips 18, 31, 34, 35, 36, 46, 55, 58, 64, and 76.*

116 Falling backward

If this fall looks familiar, you're making a couple mistakes that are conspiring to land you in the snow. This skier is only weighting his front ski, and he then makes it even more awkward by letting his body get too far behind the ski. This combination simply doesn't work. Think of that back leg as a balloon. Your body is positioned over it, and your front leg has been desperately supporting all your weight. You lean back and "pop!"—you end up deflating the back leg. You need to *use* that back leg for support instead of just trailing it behind you.

Correct this by doing two things: One, aggressively position your upper body down the hill—don't be fainthearted with your stance. Two, weight both skis evenly by keeping a tighter stance so that your back leg is underneath your hips, not dawdling uselessly. Use that back leg to push yourself forward into an energetic tele-stance. *See tips 24, 27, 31, and 49.*

117 Back ski tip dives

This is the bane of in-bounds skiers when they venture into deep soft snow for the first time. The toe baffle and sole on modern plastic boots can be so stiff that if you don't get enough weight on the back ski, the unbending boot forces the ski tip to dive, and down you go in a half-pirouette. Hard-pack skiing lets you cheat a little with that un-weighted back ski: It won't sink, so no consequences. You'll need to redefine your stance in soft snow, though, and *truly* weight that back ski. Keep that heel closer to the ski, and keep that boot under your butt. This problem was rare in the bygone era of floppy leather boots; they were simply too soft. *See tips 26, 27, 77, and 91.*

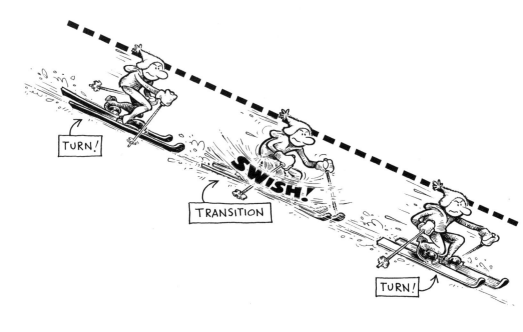

118 Not enough up and down

If you're making the transition between turns without any extension and compression, your skiing might be missing something. This is especially important if you freeze during your turn. Staying low will keep you stable, but a little up and down (extension and compression) will help your skis to rebound and deliver you into your next turn. Focus on a fluid motion—skiing is dynamic. This tip can be especially helpful to the beginner tele-skier. *See tips 11, 22, 23, 33, and 89.*

TURN!

BoING!

TRANSITION

TURN!

119 Too much up and down

Here's the follow-up (or contradiction?) to the previous tip, and it's especially important if you are driving big, fat shaped skis. If you're making the transition between turns with too much extension and compression, you are fighting against the beautiful side cut. Your shaped skis are designed to drive and carve. If you don't take advantage of this by deliberately pressuring, you are working harder than you need to. Staying low will keep you stable as you carve through each turn, while making sure to apply pressure throughout the turn. This tip can be helpful to the advanced tele-skier. *See tips 41, 42, 43, 53, and 66.*

INVOLUNTARY
PARALLEL
STANCE
MID-TELE-TURN!

120 Sneaky parallel turn

Many a lifelong alpine skier won't let go of his or her old habits. The insidious parallel turn can involuntarily sneak itself into your tele-skiing, materializing for just a micro-second in some strange places. You may have dedicated years of effort into creating parallel-turn muscle memory, and those habits are hard to break. Often you won't even know you're doing this, and it takes someone watching you to point it out. It may manifest itself only as a tiny snap: The back ski will shoot forward and then the skier will actually do the turn in the parallel mode. This is sometimes referred to as the dreaded fake-a-mark (ewww!).

Sadly, this results in the entire turn being done with the inside edge of the downhill ski while the uphill ski just trails along. This is a verboten use of a parallel behavior. The variations of this phony tele-turn are many and sometimes subtle. This situation requires a reprogramming of the skier's mind and body under the watchful eye of an instructor. A lifted heel does not a tele-turn make!

The mistake is fundamental; it's a lack of trust in the tele-position. You need to give yourself over to the tele-turn. Nothing less than complete commitment will do. *See tips 3, 7, 14, 25, 27, 40, 55, and 83.*

⟨121⟩ The broken robot

This can be the final flaw that some tele-skiers need to overcome before they have their break-through experience. Some skiers will actually do all the correct individual pieces of a tele-turn, but they'll be in separate frozen poses, like a series of still photographs. The seasoned tele-skier will watch and say, "Yikes, that robot needs some oil!" The skier will be rigid in the turn, then jerk into the transition, twitch a ski forward, and jolt back into the rigid turn position. There is something brittle and sticky going on. If there were an audio track, it would sound like a broken washing machine filled with bricks.

Each individual piece might be perfect, but they need to flow together. Imagine the difference between a frozen block of rock-hard chocolate and one that is gently thawed in a saucepan. *Become* that warm chocolate, *allow* yourself to melt into something silky and smooth. The individual pieces should meld together, in concert, as one velvety and unforced movement. Simply flow through all the pieces in a creamy liquid of delicious effortlessness. *See tips 21, 33, 38, 43, 44, 51, 66, 74, 80, and 84.*

122 Use caution when teaching your significant other

Things can get sort of tense between couples out there on the slopes. It can be a formidable challenge for couples who are used to relating on an equal basis to suddenly accept the roles of teacher and student. Sometimes it's just more sane to pay someone else for those lessons.

(123) Don't think about all these tips at once

Don't swamp your mind with every trick in this book. Overload your brain, and it'll seize up! Instead, find that *one* tip that makes the most sense for you, and practice it until it comes naturally. Then go back and find the next tip. Play with these tips–don't think of 'em as work! It's like building a house: You can only lay one brick at a time.

Good luck, tele-comrades!

About the Authors

Allen O'Bannon grew up in Portland, Oregon. While he dabbled a little in skiing and winter camping in the Cascades it was really upon moving to the mountains of Wyoming and Idaho at the end of the '80s that he began what has become a lifelong passion. Allen has worked for the National Outdoor Leadership School since 1987 and spent four seasons working for the United States Antarctic Program. He prefers cold to heat and is miserable when he thinks of global warming.

Mike Clelland never went to art school, studying *Mad Magazine* instead. Mike grew up in the flat plains of Michigan, then spent ten years (as a yuppie!) in New York City. In 1987 he thought it might be fun to be a ski bum in Wyoming for the winter. Unfortunately, after living and skiing in the Rockies, he found it quite impossible to return to his previous life in the Big City. Mike is presently living in a shed in Idaho where he divides his time between illustrator and NOLS instructor.

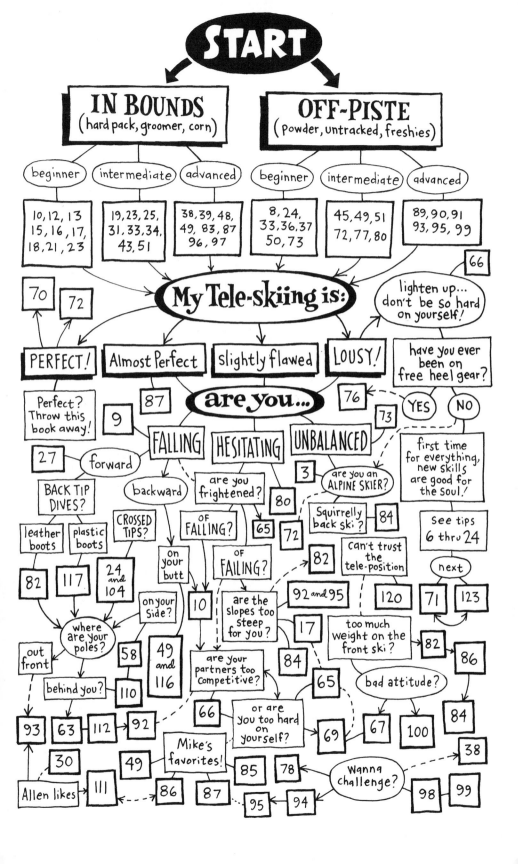

Also by Allen and Mike ...

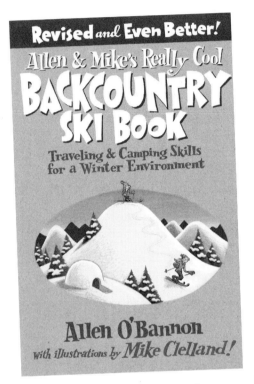